THE MANNEQUINS BEHIND THE CURTAINS

BY

JEAN P. KVAVLE

This book is a work of fiction. Places, events, and situations in this story are purely fictional. Any resemblance to actual persons, living or dead, is coincidental.

First published by AuthorHouse 05/05/04

ISBN: 1-4140-8525-7 (e-book)
ISBN: 1-4184-2704-7 (Paperback)

Library of Congress Control Number: 2004091714

This book is printed on acid free paper.

Printed in the United States of America
Bloomington, IN

CHAPTER 1

With a light-hearted whistle Amanda Leigh closed her car door, retrieved a bag of groceries from the trunk, then headed into the house. The gorgeous spring day kept her spirits soaring. It brought to mind the day of her wedding to Preston Leigh, the only man she'd ever loved. He was handsomely tall, kindly spoken and considerate, almost to a fault. Amanda adored him. Always would.

Whistling as she put away the groceries, she hurried to finish and change into her gardening shorts. She grabbed a can of cold pop, then ran through the blue carpeted living room and up the stairs to her bedroom. As she popped the can top, she saw a piece of paper on the satin bedspread. After taking a drink from the can, she put it aside, retrieving the piece of paper to read it.

Amanda,
Please forgive me for leaving you. I've been seeing another woman, whom I love. I hate to treat you like this, but I don't know how else to handle it. We'll talk later.
Preston.

Stupefied, she reread the note. Her heart raced for a brief moment then seemed to stop. She struggled to breathe, but her throat constricted. Then with a great, convulsive gasp, a rush of heaving sobs shook her body, until every muscle ached. Her heart slowly started beating again, thumping against her ribs. This can't be, she thought. I'm having some kind of horrible dream. But the piece of paper proved it was no dream. When did he write this? He had to have come home mid-morning. He knew of her plans to go out. Obviously he couldn't face her with the betrayal. Deserted! He'd deserted her? But why hadn't she seen his discontent? He showed no signs of discontent. "How could you, Preston? How could you?" she wailed.

She hugged herself, running her hands over her shivering arms. Why? Why? What woman? She crumpled the note and stared at Preston's closet door. With a tumultuous heart, she inched her way over. As she yanked at the icy knob, the door flew open to expose the dark void. An empty cave.

Her heart sank to new depths. All his clothes were gone, his shoes, and his slippers. Everything.

She tried to quiet her muddled thoughts, but with the dawning awareness of what had happened, she couldn't. "This can't be! It can't," she cried out. Rushing down the stairs, two at a time, she threw open the door to Preston's den, then stood staring at the fireplace mantle. The undeniable truth sent wrenching pains through her heart.

Where his collection of pipes usually lay, only one remained. He'd taken the other four. The pipe she'd given him for his birthday, just a few weeks ago, lay forlorn on the mantle.

She picked up the lone pipe, turning it in her hands. The smell of tobacco permeated the room, and the pipe bowl felt warm to her fingers. Had Preston smoked it while he wrote his note of betrayal? "Damn him!" she shouted to the pipe. Then with strength she didn't know she possessed, she broke the bowl from the stem and threw both parts into the fireplace ashes. Lowering her head to the mantle, tears gave way to despair. Gone now the love she'd cherished. Gone forever. She dropped to the brown leather sofa and wept, "Why? Why?"

Later, with red eyes and staggering breath, she set about doing housework, scrubbing the white-tiled kitchen floor, vacuuming the blue-carpeted stairs, washing the many- paned kitchen windows, all activities to keep her wounded mind occupied. Nothing could erase the feeling of failure that kept her throat tightened and sore, her eyes wet. What had she done to make Preston look elsewhere? She loved him with all her soul.

At first, when she found herself falling for him, she worried about the age difference. Ten years. But she soon realized it didn't matter. They loved each other. Her own father had married a woman half his age, a few years after Amanda's mother died. Only two years separated Preston from Jackie Forsythe, her stepmother.

So consumed with her apparent loss, Amanda never noticed the darkness creeping over her chilling world. Breakfast had been hours ago, and now as she worked, her stomach began to complain. Over a bowl of chicken soup and a slice of grape jelly toast, she relived that last meal with Preston.

He hadn't spoken much, not more than half a dozen words, and those mostly in response to her conversation. This wasn't so unusual. He'd never been a good conversationalist at mealtime. The one exception was the death of his parents. He blamed himself. Once he got onto that topic, he couldn't seem to get off it. She found it very troubling. What could she say to comfort him? She'd felt grateful he hadn't been with them. He might also have been killed.

Before he left for work this morning, he'd looked anxious, then asked if she was going to do the usual Friday shopping. Now she knew why. Were his clothes already packed for his fast escape? He'd come home early yesterday, while she visited a friend. Later he told her he'd taken time off to be with her, but even as he said it, it confused her. He'd seldom done that in their eight years of marriage.

Her light meal finished, Amanda made tea and sat on the seat in the kitchen bay window. Looking across the back lawn, she could barely make out the wisteria, which she had planted six years before on the bower at the fence. It had bloomed heavily this spring. Preston had sat with her, hand in hand, under it not two weeks ago. She'd never suspected his thoughts might have been on the new love, as they silently watched the crimson sunset. The sunset of their marriage, she now realized.

The invasive ringing of the phone brought her out of the emotional haze. She started to pick it up, but changed her mind. She couldn't talk to anyone right now. Gnawing apprehension of what lay ahead kept her thoughts too muddled, too unnerved, tears too close to running free.

The continuing ring jarred her troubled thoughts. She finally picked up the receiver and dropped it to dangle from the wall phone. An angry voice came over the line. "What the hell took you so long?" The unpleasant, piercing words followed her across the room like menacing arrows. She turned back, grabbed the receiver, hung it up momentarily, and then dropped it to dangle free again. She'd recognized her father's voice. A man who couldn't be reasoned with under the best of circumstances.

Deep in agony of spirit, she dragged herself up the spiral stairs to her bed, but lay awake silently crying. After sleepless hours of misery, she played tapes of her stepmother's recitals. Jackie played the harp with the talent of an angel. Three tapes finished before she drifted into a fitful sleep, frequently punctuated by the words in Preston's note, "I've been seeing another woman, whom I love."

Daylight came too soon. Amanda lay attempting to sort over her options. Try as she might, no resolution came to her bone-weary mind. It's too early, she thought, maybe tomorrow or next week. Maybe Preston just wanted some time alone to work out his problem. He can't have left me like this, without some regrets, some feelings of guilt. He'll probably come back in a day or two, then we'll work it out. A new hope kept her from giving into her profound sorrow. Without an ounce of energy, she pulled herself into a sitting position and headed for a hot shower. Something to soothe and relax her.

Fifteen minutes later, she collected the morning mail and newspaper. Though her body no longer ached, her stomach felt queasy.

She sat at the round table in the alcove, sipping tea. In the mail she found a bill from the local jeweler, Preston's friend. Puzzled, she opened it. The bill was substantial, but it didn't state the purchase. Preston hadn't bought any jewelry for almost a year. Not since her last birthday. A chilling thought crossed her mind. Was this for his new love? Her hands grew cold and clammy. For two hours she paced about the house, killing time until the jewelry store opened. Then she called.

"Michael, this is Amanda. We received a bill this morning. What was it for?"

After a pause, he replied, "Preston said it was to be a surprise. I can't tell you."

Incensed, she demanded, "Did he take it with him, or have it sent?" She'd never liked this man. He seemed too sleazy for her, too fawning.

"I can't tell you that, either. I'm sorry, Amanda."

"Suit yourself," she said, finding it hard to contain her anger. "But Preston is away and will be for some time. If you want payment before next Easter, you'd better tell me where it was sent, or I don't pay." She wanted to kick the man. To send a bill and not state what for. Such gall!

After a moment, he replied, "It was delivered by messenger."

"To whom?"

"I'm not at liberty to say. I'm sorry."

"What was it?"

He hesitated again. "I can't tell you, Amanda. I'm sorry. I promised Preston."

"Sorry, my foot," she replied. "Thank you anyway." She slammed down the receiver. "Preston can pay for it. I'll never write a check for that," she shouted to the mute walls.

She wanted to know where Preston had gone. To a hotel? An apartment? The new love's home? With trembling hands, she picked up the phone and dialed his office. They might know, and she had to find out.

"Why, he's moved to London. Didn't you go with him?" the startled receptionist asked. Preston and his business partner Cole Martin were importers of Oriental statuary and art pieces, with overseas offices in Hong Kong and London. So, the new love lives in London. Why else would he have headed there? No, he won't be coming back in a day or two. All hope gone, she leaned her head against the window. Why had he turned from her? She'd always done her best to be the wife he wanted. He'd never complained about anything. So what went wrong?

The jangling phone interrupted her thoughts. She resented the intrusion, but answered anyway.

"How are you this morning?" Pauline asked. Preston's sister sounded too friendly to be natural. She almost always resented Amanda, and treated her accordingly.

"Fine," Amanda replied, her voice sounding as dead as her heart felt.

"Something wrong?" Now Pauline talked with a lilt in her voice. Was she smiling?

Amanda replied, "I'm just tired this morning. Don't mind me."

"Want to go shopping, later?" Pauline had inherited a great deal of money. Shopping filled her leisure hours. If she had any hobbies, Amanda didn't know about them, nor did Pauline ever before ask Amanda to go shopping.

"I'm tied up today, Pauline. Another time. OK?" She knew the invitation would never come again, which pleased her.

Several seconds passed before Pauline answered, "You sound as if you're in a bad mood." She abruptly hung up.

Amanda stared at the phone for a second. She had the feeling Pauline knew what had happened. Had Preston told her? Confided in her? She closed her eyes in anguish, tears running freely down her cheeks.

CHAPTER 2

Unrelenting guilt weighed like a shroud over Preston's mind on his flight to London. He'd left home the day before to spend a miserable night waiting in the airport hotel. And now as the plane neared Heathrow, he felt again the anguish of having betrayed Amanda. He was a traitor and a coward. Unable to face her, he'd left a short note. How could he have been so cruel? Or for that matter, have put himself in a situation where, whichever direction he jumped, he'd hurt someone. It was a trap he'd unwittingly fallen into.

Bitterness filled him. He tried to put his actions in true prospective. Amanda had been a loyal and loving wife. A considerate one.

Forget her, a voice inside his head kept saying. You're off on a completely new adventure, as Jackie had laughingly explained it, after the decision to move to London had been made. She'd arranged for the hotel, a place to stay while they hunted for a permanent home. She'd even made the flight arrangements, then cleverly left the week before Preston on a "shopping" trip to Paris. She would be waiting for him in the London hotel.

The whole crazy business had started on the second anniversary of his parents' deaths a few weeks ago. A bitter sense of neglected responsibility gnawed at Preston's conscience. If he'd driven them to Boise to visit their friends, the accident might never have happened. This guilt had put him in a mournful mood. He'd tried to discuss it with Amanda, but she'd busied herself and didn't seem to be listening. He'd needed reassurance that he wasn't to blame, though his sister Pauline had accused him of being selfish not to have driven them. Not that she'd ever done anything for their parents.

On that same morning, Pauline had visited his office, guessing he'd be depressed. She stayed with him through lunch, but wasn't particularly sympathetic.

"Why keep hashing it over?" she'd asked. "What's done is done. You made a mistake, that's all there is to it."

He'd paced most of the afternoon, his black mood deepening, matching the churning storm blowing outside his window. But just before closing time, Jackie, wearing a scoop-necked dress and high heels, breezed in to say hello. She laughed as she entered his office. Before that moment laughter had seemed unattainable. But soon her charming ways pushed back the darkness in his mind. She made him forget his shortcomings. He told her he had always admired her strength, her charm, and her easy manner. Now he wondered why he'd said that.

Jackie then readily confessed, "We often make love in my dreams," she'd said. "Both wanting each other so desperately. In my dreams I want you more than anything else."

Not believing one word of it, he'd said, "But they are just dreams." Yet it did boost his ego. Then when he looked out the window, the old black mood dropped back like a smothering blanket. Heavy sheets of rain pounded against the glass, distorting everything. "I hate driving the freeway in this foul weather," he said bleakly.

"Then why do it? You have an apartment here in town for business guests, and I don't have my car. So why not let's use it? Call Amanda and explain that you don't like to drive in such rain. She'll understand. Anyway, Milo is away, as you already know." She had married Milo Forsythe, Amanda's father, two years after his first wife died. He was forty-nine, she just twenty-four. Amanda, then twelve, was an active child and seemed constantly underfoot. Jackie instructed the nanny to keep Amanda away from the adults.

"I can't do that to Amanda. What if she finds out?" Preston asked. He half wanted to stay in town with Jackie, but uneasiness gripped him. He'd never done anything like this before.

Jackie laughed at his troubled expression. "But that's the point. We don't tell her, or anyone. We'll just have some drinks sent up. Cheer each other. Avoid a lonely night. That's all. I'll sleep on the couch. No harm done."

A night of laughter seemed a welcome change right now. What could be the harm in that? Maybe it would help ease his feelings of guilt over his parents' deaths.

At dinner his conscience began prickling, but as the evening wore on, and after a few drinks, he began to relax. As they talked, and drank, Jackie seemed more and more desirable, flirting, cajoling, and finally embracing him in a demanding kiss. He couldn't say he'd tried to reject her advances, though they'd flustered him at first. But soon he began to accept them, invite them. As she slipped out of her clothes, his hands found her body smooth, warm and inviting. He now was eager for her. They made love several times before Jackie slept in his arms, exhausted, but smiling like an angel. He slept little, suddenly swept with guilt and unable to justify his actions. He could barely face Amanda in the days that followed, for the affair continued. He couldn't seem to free himself of Jackie, and in those tender moments of lovemaking, he didn't want to. She'd become a compulsion.

Now as the plane started to descend, he remembered he'd sent Jackie pearls. Oh hell, he thought suddenly, I didn't stop at the jewelers and pay for them. Now Amanda will get the bill. He felt ill. He could have spared her that, at least.

He'd been too weak to reject Jackie's advances, and the full realization made him sick in mind and spirit as the plane coasted down the runway.

From Heathrow to the hotel, the cabby prattled on about the miserable weather. To Preston it seemed not much different from a Seattle downpour, so he ignored the chatter, except to grunt or nod at what seemed appropriate times.

He thought longingly again of Jackie. She had the svelte body of a thirty-year old woman, though she had gained her forties. Her dark eyes always seemed to be dancing, but could darken with excitement. Her dark hair, kept short and curly, was soft and fragrant. He loved to run his fingers through it. Her mouth against his made him forget everything. He knew she'd had affairs, and now wondered if he was just another name on her list? A long list of diversions from a marriage to a much older man? A boring existence for one as lovely as Jackie.

When he reached the hotel, Jackie wasn't there. He walked through the suite, opening the closet to inspect it. Jackie's clothes, gowns, cocktail dresses and suits hung to one side, leaving room for his clothes. Suddenly short of breath, and almost in a panic, he dashed for the phone to call Amanda. As he lifted the receiver, he heard the click of a key in the door. Hand trembling, he replaced the phone. He turned to face Jackie, his heart pounding like a pneumatic hammer. He could barely hear her enthusiastic, "Preston, my darling. You've finally arrived."

Milo, sporting an expansive stomach that hid any sign of hips, had recently resorted to wearing suspenders. He still dressed as if going to the office, though he'd sold his business when he retired a year ago. Because traveling caused his ample body too much discomfort, he stayed at home while Jackie took her pleasure trips abroad. This time the lure of Paris, and a shopping spree, had drawn her away. He hated it when she was gone, but he could do nothing about it. He didn't want to lose her, but he felt damned lonely with her gone. Each time she left, he worried. Her many adulterous affairs kept him uneasy.

Jackie had been away a week, and he expected a call from her that should have come days ago. This time she hadn't told him where she intended to stay, so he couldn't call her. He thought it odd at the time, but she explained, "I'm not sure. I'd like to try a different hotel. One a little more private." She continued to pack as she talked.

"You might well end up without a room," he'd cautioned.

She'd scoffed, "It's worth risking." She all but ignored his presence, her back turned to him.

"There's always a first time," he replied.

Then when she left, she'd given him a passing kiss on the cheek and hurried out to the waiting cab. Milo had wanted to drive her to Sea-Tac, but she insisted he'd be wasting most of the day. Better to play golf with his friends.

But Milo hadn't contacted his friends. He'd stayed home to sit in the den and worry. One thing for sure, she'd never just walk away without his knowing. She would always have to come back for her harp. She'd often told him she couldn't live without it. He resented the time she spent with it, ignoring him for hours on end. Still, when they made love, all worries drifted away just as mists evaporate in brilliant sunshine. He adored his angel.

As he sat reading the evening paper, his housekeeper Agatha Thatcher opened the den door. Milo looked up as she poked her head in the opening.

"What you wanting for dinner?" The dour-faced Agatha asked, posed more as a command than a question. She had been Milo's housekeeper since Amanda's birth. It was obvious to Milo that she never liked Jackie, though she never spoke of it.

Milo looked thoughtfully at her, eyes squinting. "Has Jackie called?"

Agatha shook her head, the corners of her mouth curling slightly. "Not once. Having too good a time, I suppose." Her watery blue eyes seemed to smile with satisfaction.

"What about dinner?"

"To hell with that. I couldn't eat anything." He watched her turn away shaking her head. He knew what she thought, and he determined not to give her the satisfaction of changing his mind.

But before she closed the door, she said, "Let me know when you decide otherwise."

"I won't," he called after her. Yet he knew he probably would.

Unable to get his mind off Jackie, he went to the phone and dialed Amanda. As soon as she answered, he said, "Tell me where Jackie went."

After a moment's hesitation, Amanda replied, "You said she went to Paris. I only know what you told me."

Dissatisfied, he grumped, "Well, I'm sure she told you more than she told me." He knew it wasn't likely because Jackie and Amanda had never hit it off, often at odds over one trifling thing or another.

"Not on your life! She never talks to me, only at me."

"That's mostly your fault," he chided. "You never tried to understand her."

"And you think you do?"

Milo sighed and ran his index finger up and down the underside of one of his navy-blue suspenders. “Well, I hate eating alone. Come over for dinner tonight. Preston can stand me a game of chess.” For several moments Amanda never spoke. “You still there?” he asked.

“Yes. Sorry, but we have other arrangements.” Her voice seemed strained, but he ignored it.

“Whatever it is, cancel it.” He softened his voice now. “Give your poor old dad a little attention.” This usually worked, and it made him feel good. She’d come sure enough.

She replied, “Another time, perhaps, but not tonight.” Her voice held an edge of contempt, and he resented it.

“It’s tonight I need you.”

“Sorry,” she replied, “Another time.”

He slammed down the receiver and yelled out, “Agatha!”

By God, he thought, I’ll not eat alone again. When Agatha came in, he said, “Let’s have pork chops for dinner. Haven’t had them for a long time. We’ll eat in here. You and me.” That will burn Jackie, he thought. Servants belong in the kitchen, she always maintained. At the moment, he didn’t care what she’d think.

Her forehead frowned, but Agatha’s lips softened into a hint of a smile. “Not pork chops,” she replied. “You’re not to eat pork. Doctor’s orders. Remember?”

“The blasted doctor doesn’t live here. What are you going to do? Tell him?” He wished she’d just do as she was told.

“Of course not. I’ll broil lamb chops.”

She turned as Milo replied, “I asked for pork chops.”

Slowly shaking her head, she replied, “Would you rather have ground turkey meat loaf?”

He sighed in disgust. “Make it lamb chops. But I want mint sauce with them.” He knew she only considered his health, when she acted this way.

“Mint sauce and one lamb chop,” she replied with a smile. “And lots of veggies.”

CHAPTER 3

After Amanda left the phone she sat on the kitchen window seat, looking out across the back yard. Eight years she'd lived here with Preston. Eight wasted years. Now she'd have to start over, build some sort of life for herself. But what? How? She didn't even know if she could.

She'd never held a permanent job. Never been completely independent, on her own. Faced with the prospect now, it frightened her. One fact she knew for a certainty. Too many memories of good times here would never let her remain. Preston had owned the house before she married him. Though she'd loved the place, she never felt the house belonged to her, always thinking of it as Preston's house. It would always remain Preston's house.

She walked out the back door to stand a few moments on the lush lawn, then she made her way to the arbor. The bench under the shade of the wisteria felt cold as she sat down. No more magical sunsets with Preston. No more hand holding, no more kisses, and no more loving nights. As much as she wanted to, she realized she could change nothing. Everything had changed without any effort on her part.

Amanda hadn't told her father or Pauline about the desertion, though she suspected Pauline knew. Because Pauline's mind didn't function normally, to face her yet was unthinkable. Perhaps in a week or two. And as for her father, she knew what he'd say no matter what she did. She'd never done anything to suit him, and she didn't intend to start now. No way!

A breeze arose, fluttering the arbor leaves. It chilled her, raising goose bumps on her sleeveless arms. As she returned to the house, she paused long enough to look at the flowerbeds she'd taken so much pride in. Weed seedlings were poking up everywhere. Now would be the perfect time to pull them, roots and all. But she just stood looking at them. She wouldn't pull them, nor would she cut the dead blooms from the roses. She had no will to keep up the house or yard of the man who had betrayed her. Dead, that's what she felt, dead in body and spirit, only a numbed mind to guide her, tell her how to cope, what to do.

Preston had been in London for over a week, and Jackie felt his discontent. She'd awakened to find him standing before the window. Twice she'd spoken to him, but he hadn't heard her. "For heaven's sake, darling. What's the matter?" She went to him, putting her arms around his neck and drawing his face down to her own. She kissed him, then lowered her hands to rub them over his hairy chest. "Come back to bed," she urged. "Make love to me." The anguish on his face, and in his eyes, made her breath catch in her throat.

"You go back to bed," he replied. "No need for both of us to lose sleep." He kissed her on the forehead, removed her hands from his chest and turned her toward the bed. "I'll be all right in a few minutes."

Jackie slipped under the covers, but lay watching him. She adored this new love more than any of the others. He's much to good for a milquetoast like Amanda, she told herself. Amanda with her conventional thinking, conventional ways, conventional clothes. Why he stayed with her for eight years, I'll never know. Even Milo thought his daughter spineless, in a conventional way of course. Not enough sense or ambition to go after what she wanted, allowing chance to dictate her direction in life. Well, Jackie defended her own actions, I get what I want, and I want Preston.

She slipped from the covers, let her silk gown drop to the floor, then with the melodic voice of an angel, said, "Darling Preston. Let me give you what you need to make you sleep." She moved her hands over his body, caressing seductively.

Within moments, both were in bed, and very soon Preston slept, but not Jackie. During the heavy love making, Preston had called her Amanda. Had it been a slip of the tongue, or unspoken desire? Sleep avoided her for hours.

Pauline dialed Amanda's number and waited. No answer. "Well, she's still sulking over her loss," she said aloud. "But everyone can't win in this game. Too bad Amanda had to lose." She thought for a moment, then laughed. "Poor Milo. He doesn't even know what's happened, nor that he's a winner. Of course Preston loses, but so what." Again she laughed.

Pauline had always had a crush on Preston's partner Cole Martin. But she'd had a couple of bouts with a mental illness Preston considered serious enough for her never to marry. She disagreed. "Doctors don't know everything," she'd told him. As far as she knew, Preston had told no one about it, not even Cole, though he threatened to, if she continued to pursue him.

She had laughed at her brother, and with her friends had hatched the plot he'd recently carried out. Unwittingly, of course, but still the finger would never point at her. And now without any interference, for Preston would be living in London, she intended to have a complete makeover, shop for expensive and fashionable clothes, and have her hair styled, and perhaps dyed. She'd become a completely new woman, a sophisticated woman, one Cole would be mad over as soon as he saw her.

She'd play hard to get, at first, but slowly she'd pretend to accept his attentions. Perhaps they'd even make love before she rejected him. Make him sorry he hadn't wanted her before.

She remembered his divorce, how she'd made up excuses to see him, sympathize with him. At first he'd seemed flattered, but after their first date, a dance, she'd overheard him tell a mutual friend, "She's a nice kid, but she clings like glue. Couldn't get out of her sight for a moment."

"I'll show him," Pauline now shouted. "Make him ache to have me. Never want me out of his sight. And I'll be laughing the whole time."

She turned to her friends, the clothing store mannequins, who were lazing about the room, some on their backs gazing at the ceiling, some sitting on the floor, their backs against the wall.

"With your advice we've won," she told them. "I'll buy you more chocolates as a reward."

"It's about time," they all agreed.

Still unable to think clearly, Amanda called her best friend Brooke Conners for advice. It was early Saturday morning, but Brooke immediately answered the phone.

"It's me," Amanda said, her voice quivering.

"Well, so you're still alive, my friend?" Brooke sounded as if she were smiling.

"Of course," Amanda shot back. "Are you busy today? Anything planned?"

"No. What's up?"

"I need someone to talk to. A long talk."

"I'm your gal. When can you get here?"

"Probably about one."

"You'll stay overnight, of course."

"I'd love to."

Brooke laughed. "Then I guess I'll get up."

"I'm sorry. Did I wake you?"

"No. I was just reading some briefs. Delaying that shower. Is Preston away?"

Amanda hesitated before saying, "Yes, for good."

"Wow! Then this is serious talk?"

"He's left me for another woman. Ran off to London to be with her." Because tears had come to her eyes, she wanted to cut the conversation short. "Look, I'll be leaving in ten minutes."

"You remember I've moved, don't you?"

"Yes. I have your new address and a Portland map."

"Good. Drive carefully. You know what the freeway is like on weekends."

"See you about one." She hung up, feeling as close to tears as she had been for days. But the prospect of talking to Brooke cheered her. The two had gone through high school and college together, though Amanda had quit at the end of her junior year to marry Preston. Brooke had gone on to earn her degree in law. She now had an excellent job as a corporate lawyer in Portland, Oregon.

Brooke had been raised in a dysfunctional family and vowed never to marry. She had never known a day without her parents fighting, some of the fights horrible and brutal. Amanda didn't believe Brooke would keep that vow, but somehow she had managed to.

Amanda hurried to throw a few items into her overnight case. Soon she was on her way to Portland, arriving just before one.

Brooke, bare-footed and wearing a red and black wrap-around dress, opened the door before Amanda could ring the bell. She stood tall and willowy, with short blond hair. A contagious smile played about her mouth. "Gee, you're just in time for lunch." She stepped aside for Amanda to enter.

"Good. What are we having?" Amanda dropped her case to the floor, then hugged her friend.

"Homemade tacos. I've learned to cook," she proudly bragged. Both laughed as Brooke led the way to the kitchen.

Amanda looked around. "You did buy a large house, much larger than it sounded when you described it over the phone. But it's beautiful. One I'd love to have."

"Let's eat, then I'll show you the place. And you can tell me all about your problem."

With a sigh, Amanda replied, "It's one I can't seem to get a hold on. But that can wait." She sat at a round table, which was covered with a white linen cloth, while Brooke stirred contents in a pan on the stove. The lettuce, tomatoes and cheese were already on the table. Soon they were assembling tacos.

"How's your work going?" Amanda asked between bites.

"Great! I love it. Gives me a better perspective on life in general."

"My, that sounds impressive."

"It's not, really." She paused. "Helps me see both sides of an argument. Like looking out from the mirror as well as looking in."

Amanda supposed Brooke was talking about her own family, so didn't comment. Brooke had never fully explained about her family problems, her allusions to them generally veiled. And Amanda had too much respect for Brooke to pry.

"I could never do that before. I find it comforting."

"Wish I had that ability. I certainly can't understand Preston's reasons, but then he never explained them."

When they finished eating, Brooke gave a tour of the old house located in the Laurelhurst section of Portland. The rooms were large, but peeling wallpaper disfigured them. The living room fireplace had a huge oak mantel, and the fire irons beside it were shiny black, obviously new. The paint on the doors and trim was rough, as if several layers had been piled on top of others.

Upstairs, old maple trees shaded all the bedroom windows. The master bedroom had just been freshly painted in a pale blue. "Did I ever have a job scraping off the old paint," Brook complained. The new lace curtains were pulled back with a tie. The four windows had nine small panes each. And between two of the windows, on the outside wall, stood a pink limestone fireplace with a wide hearth. "Bet you love this room," Amanda volunteered.

"Yes, and I did all the work myself. I'll probably have to have some help with other things, like painting the outside. But for the most part, I intend to refinish it."

Standing in admiration, Amanda said, "You've done a good job. I admire you, but then you were always very capable."

Brooke laughed. "Never mind the admiration, let's go down to the den and you can tell me what happened."

Seated comfortably, Amanda explained exactly what had happened. "I'm at a loss. I've been hit in the stomach, hard, and I can't seem to catch my breath again," she concluded.

Looking puzzled, Brooke asked, "Just like that? He walked out without one word. That son-of-a... He's gone soft in the head."

"And I have no idea why, nor who the woman is, nor what I should do."

"Do you think he'll come back when he..."

"No," Amanda cut in. "He's moved to London to be with her."

Shrugging, Brooke said, "I'd never have believed he'd do such a thing, not after the way he chased you."

"Nor I, but it goes to show you never really know."

"File for divorce, and don't let the other woman live in luxury. Take most of what he's got."

She'd avoided thinking about it, but knew she had to face the prospect. "I guess so," Amanda replied.

"That's not very convincing."

Amanda stood and began pacing in circles around the room, trying to think clearly. "I don't want to skin him, but what's the point of remaining married, under the circumstances?"

"None. If Preston loves the other woman, he'll want out, but you'd better come to some understanding about finances," Brooke advised. "And quickly. Get yourself a good attorney. Not one of his friends."

"I know, but it all seems so cruel. So unjust."

"Forget justice. It seldom, if ever, exists." Amanda remained silent, so Brooke continued. "If I were you, I'd get a divorce and start over. You're still young, and no children are involved."

"Is that legal or friendly advice?"

"A bit of both. The man no longer wants you, and you could never again trust him." She watched Amanda pacing.

"No, but first I've got to find out who the other woman is. What drew Preston to her." She stopped pacing and sat down again.

"What for? It won't make any difference in the long run."

"Probably not, but I've got to do it."

"That's crazy. If you want my opinion, don't have anything further to do with him."

"It probably is crazy, but I've got to find out. I'll pry his address out of Cole, his partner, who no doubt knows." She leaned her elbows on her knees. "What about you? No love interest?"

Brooke smiled, the dimples in both cheeks becoming evident. "You know better than to ask. My parents hated each other after only a few years of marriage. Eventually they both found other loves, but not until they made my life miserable. Always trying to make me choose between them. That's not for me, though I'd love to have a couple of kids." She eyed Amanda with an amused smile.

Wide-eyed, Amanda stared. "Got the father picked out?"

"I don't need to know the father. I want to adopt. There are so many children without parents these days. Abused kids, abandoned kids, you name it. They're all over the place. I'd like to make life better for a couple of them. Give them a real chance at life, without bickering parents." The last words were said with a tinge of anger.

Speechless, Amanda stared for several seconds. Then she said, "What a wonderful idea. Go for it. When will you start?"

"I want to get the house fixed up first. Bring them into a clean, bright home."

"How long will that take?"

"I expect to be finished with what I can do by fall. I'll have to work fast, but that's OK. In the meantime, I'll have the outside painted, and the carpets replaced."

"I could help," Amanda volunteered. "I could come down on Friday nights. Stay over until Monday morning."

"What about your place?"

"It's not my place. It's Preston's place. He can look after it. I'll get a small apartment for the time being."

"And then what?" Brooke asked.

"Go back to school and get my degree. Start that new life Preston forced on me. Why, someday I might even thank him." She sounded far more confident than she felt, but perhaps if she kept pounding away at it, it might work. She could come out on top of it all. "In the meantime, I'm off to London to meet this husband stealer, and to give Preston a piece of my mind about the way he left."

"You'll regret it, unless I miss my guess."

"So be it," Amanda replied, a lump beginning to form in her throat as Brooke's caveat registered in her mind.

CHAPTER 4

Jackie sat plucking at the strings of a cut-off tennis racket, her way of keeping healthy calluses on her fingertips. Preston had gone to work. Lately he'd spent a great deal of time at work and it concerned her, not so much at his being gone, but because she suspected Amanda filled his thoughts. He'd called her Amanda more than once.

She'd be the first to admit he'd treated Amanda badly, never hinting at what he intended to do. Jackie, at the time, felt he'd be better off without a dramatic scene. That's how she'd handled it with her own husband Milo. "If we don't tell them, they can't complain," she'd said, feeling confidently smug about it. Now she realized she'd have to face the inevitable scene with Milo. How else could she get her harp? He'd never send it to her, balking at the expense. He'd done so when she wanted to replace her old one. This one was a tenth anniversary present from Milo. She missed it terribly. After all, she'd played in the symphony orchestra for years, even making recordings of her efforts.

Suddenly she remembered having promised Milo she'd never again take a lover. That was the condition under which the new harp had been purchased. She'd managed to keep a few affairs from him, but Preston wasn't simply another affair. She intended to marry him. But would Milo see it that way? With a shake of the head, she knew she'd have to scheme to get the harp. Milo had given it to her, so it was hers.

When Preston came home, she'd ask him to help her devise a plan to get the harp. Of course Preston could buy her a new one, but would he? Not at the moment. Not while he kept thinking of Amanda.

Amanda had made arrangements to see Cole, though she had to argue with him to get the appointment. He smiled and stood as she entered his office.

"How are you, Amanda?" he asked, offering his hand at the same time. Of medium height, he wore the usual business suit of dark blue.

"I'm fine, I suppose, under the circumstances."

"Please sit down." He motioned to the chair beside his desk. When she was seated, he said, "What can I do for you?"

"I need the answers to a few questions. Other than yourself, I don't know who has the answers." She placed her purse on the floor beside the chair, then looked up at him.

"Amanda, I find betraying a confidence very distasteful. I want you to know that," he said, removing a handkerchief from his pocket to wipe his moist brow.

"I'm sure you do," she replied, "but I've got to contact Preston. A divorce is inevitable, so I need to know what he wants done with the house. It's his and he should take care of it. Sell it, whatever he wants, only I'm not going to do any more gardening, mowing of the lawn, watering, none of the things he expected me to do before. The whole place can dry up and blow away, as far as I'm concerned. I'll be out of it just as soon as I can find another place to live."

Cole shook his head. "You're too hasty," he cautioned. "Slow down." He leaned foreword, his arms on the desk.

"Preston didn't slow down when he took a lover, or left me for her." Deep resentment filled her as she spoke. "He took the coward's way out."

"Amanda..." he hesitated, "I'm not so sure this new romance will last."

"I don't care if they both go to hell. I want out of the marriage. He destroyed it." Even as she spoke, she realized being angry with Cole helped no one. "Try to understand," she said, in softer tones.

He nodded. "Yes."

He made no further comment, so she continued. "I have to know where Preston is, besides just in London." She had intended to tell him of her plans to go to London, but thought better of it. "I have to know where to send a letter. No postal service is good enough to deliver a letter addressed to Preston Leigh in London."

"You intend to write to him?"

She nodded. "Of course. All I need is the address."

He opened his desk drawer. "I'll see what I can do. Perhaps the office address?"

She shook her head. "And have his secretary open and read it? No way! That makes for juicy office scuttlebutt."

"But if you address it to his home, the new love might open and read it," he cautioned.

"Then she'll get her ears burned, won't she?"

With a sigh, he said, "Anger won't resolve this, you know." His brown eyes squinted as if he didn't know what to do.

"Nor will time," she shot back. "He betrayed me. I can never again trust him. Ever!"

"Amanda..." He paused, rubbing his mouth with stiff fingers. "These things happen. Middle-age syndrome. That doesn't mean he's quit loving you."

She jumped to her feet. "What? Well, isn't that just too bad." She tried to control her anger by taking a deep breath, then sat down again. "Oh, Cole," she added more gently, "You've no idea what this has done to me. I don't think I'll ever trust a man again."

"You will, Amanda. Just give yourself time." He opened his desk drawer wider and looked down at it, then looked up at Amanda. "How soon will you be writing to him?"

She realized he intended to contact Preston. "Just as soon as you give me the address," she replied, leaning foreword in anticipation.

Preston, on his walk home from the office, was plagued by uncertainty. He couldn't get his mind on settling down in London. Jackie kept pressuring him, but he had no desire or ambition to hunt for a house. Thinking of the house back in Kent, Washington, his heart sank. That was the one house he wanted to live in. But he couldn't. Not now. Any court would award it to Amanda in a divorce action. She should rightfully have it anyway, after what he'd done. What would she be doing now? It was almost ten in the morning there. She'd be cleaning the house, or shopping, or perhaps gardening. He recalled how she always kept the lawn and gardens spotless. But no matter how much work she did during the day, dinner was always on the table at six.

A few minutes later, he entered his hotel suite. Jackie sat strumming silently on the strings of a tennis racket. She looked wistfully at him. Was she, too, having second thoughts? Perhaps thinking of Milo?

He removed his jacket and dropped it to the back of a chair.

"Well, don't you say hello anymore?" She set the racket aside and went to him. Her arms slid around his neck as she stood on tiptoe to kiss him.

He found himself returning the kiss automatically, embracing her for only a moment as his thoughts slipped back to Amanda.

"Bad day?" she asked, stepping aside to study him. "You look almost grouchy."

The question brought his thoughts back. "No. Everything's just fine." He forced a smile.

"Who do you think you're kidding?"

"I'm not trying to kid anyone," he replied. He kissed her on top of her head, then removed his tie and plopped down on the overstuffed chair.

As she looked at him, her expression relaxed into a smile. "I could use your help with something," she began. "That's if you're up to it. Not in a bad mood?" She lowered her chin and raised her eyes in a pleading manner.

"Try me and see," he replied, forcing himself to sound natural.

"We'll, it's like this." She sat at his feet, looking up adoringly, her amber-flecked eyes studying his face. "You see, I'm lost without my harp. I can't figure out how to get it here. Would you help me devise a plan to get Milo to ship it?"

"What?" He hadn't been listening closely, his mind again on the way he'd treated Amanda.

She brightened. "Of course I could always buy a new one here, let Milo sell the old one. But I'm fond of it."

"Buy a new one?" he asked. "With what? I deposited most of my ready cash in an account for Amanda."

"Why did you do that?" Her voice sounded accusatory.

"I couldn't leave her without funds," he replied.

She stared at him. "I don't mean your money, silly. I've still got credit cards."

He couldn't believe it. She'd left Milo without one word, and now she wanted to charge a new harp to his account.

"He's loaded. He'll never miss the pittance."

Angered at her lack of conscience, he said, "It's about time you let him know what you've done."

"I've done? What about you?"

He pondered on it a moment. "It was the coward's way out, but I at least left a note."

"We're two of a kind you know, so don't point your finger at me."

"I'm not." He stood, turning away from her.

"Really?" she shot back.

He knew he deserved her anger. "I've been thinking about what I've done. I could have handled the situation differently with Amanda. The same with you and Milo."

"So now I'm at fault." Red-faced, she stood, picked up the tennis racket and slammed it into the magazine rack, where she kept it.

"Of course I didn't mean that." He wondered why she was always so touchy. He couldn't mention Amanda without Jackie getting angered. He couldn't remember the last time he'd angered Amanda. It had happened so seldom. "Where would you like to eat tonight?" he asked, tired of the tenseness between them.

"Anywhere, just as long as you don't bring Amanda with us."

He stared at her for a moment, then went to the bathroom and closed the door. No, Amanda never kept him on the defensive. Never. He stripped and stepped into the shower.

Normally, he spent about three minutes in the shower, but he had no desire to get out of this one. Closing his eyes, he let the warm water cascade over his body, wishing the comfort to his body could be transferred to his mind. He put his head under the shower in an effort to wash the guilt away. It felt wonderful for a few minutes, but as soon as he dried himself, the guilt returned. Nothing could wash that from his mind. "My God! What have I done?"

Amanda received a call just as she got into bed. Who would call at this hour? she thought.

Pauline said, "Just wanted to tell you I'm all packed for my trip tomorrow." The words sounded breathy, as if she had been working hard.

"Trip?" Amanda knew nothing about a planned trip. Was Pauline going to visit Preston?

"My first real shopping spree. All by myself."

"Where are you headed? Paris?"

"New York first, then perhaps Paris. I'm terribly excited."

"I'll bet," Amanda replied. "What are you shopping for?"

"Dresses, suits, coats, the usual."

To Amanda, the spur-of-the-moment trip was anything but usual. And shopping for a completely new wardrobe certainly couldn't be called usual. "When did you decide this?"

"The moment Preston left for London. It feels wonderful to finally have him out of my hair." The response came quickly. "I just waited until now to be sure Preston wasn't coming back."

Amanda blinked in disbelief. Then Pauline had known all along of Preston's intentions. Why hadn't she given some hint of what was to come? Amanda had never particularly liked Preston's sister, and wanted now to end the conversation. "Hope you have a nice trip," she said. "Good-bye."

She hung up, anger building inside her again. Tomorrow she'd make plans for a trip to London. Surprise Preston, and find out the name of his paramour.

As she settled down again, the front door bell rang. "What now?" she grumbled. She slipped into a robe and hurried down the stairs barefoot. Once the porch light lit up the dark, she looked through the peephole.

On the steps stood two older women, waiting and smiling whimsically, as if pulling some sort of trick. They were dressed alike, same straw hats, plain shirts, blue jeans and cowboy boots. Twins? "Oh, no," Amanda breathed.

She opened the door, but before she could speak, the two women chirped, "Surprise. We told Preston one of these days we'd surprise him. You must be Amanda."

Oh, yes, Preston's aunts from Bozeman, Montana. "Come in," she said, her tight voice catching in her throat. She stepped back to let them enter.

"Sorry we're so late in arriving. I'm Molly. And this is Hallie," she said, turning to her sister.

Amanda, confused and flustered, led them to the living room. She felt at a loss for words. The twins dropped their luggage beside the sofa and sat down.

"We thought we'd never get here. Took ages," Hallie explained. "Sorry we're so late in arriving. Where is Preston?"

"He's in London."

They stared at her, then each other. "For how long?" Molly asked. The two removed their hats and dropped them on the coffee table.

"I don't know." She wanted to tell them what had happened, but not this soon after their arrival.

With a hurt frown, Hallie said, "That's mighty inconsiderate of him." She shook her head as if not quite understanding how it could have happened. The twins were identical, except for the parting of hair. Hallie's was parted on the left, Molly's parted in the middle.

They had rather large noses and generous mouths, circled with the telltale lines brought on by their good humor.

"You're welcome to stay," Amanda volunteered, knowing they would be tired. Feeling helpless, she wondered how she could now go to London. She felt this visit would be an extended one.

The women looked at each other, frowning, then Hallie spoke up. "This isn't just a visit; Preston and Pauline are our only living relatives. We wanted to be closer to Preston. We had hoped we could live here while we hunt for a house. Maybe a month or two."

Amanda swallowed before she spoke. "Of course. You're welcome to stay as long as you want." The words almost choked her. "You must be tired. Are you hungry?"

"I'm too tuckered to think about food," Hallie answered. "We've been traveling since dawn."

"Come on, then. I'll show you to your room." Amanda led the way, all the while struggling to stop from crying at the turn of events. Why did they have to come now, after Preston had deserted her? Hallie and Molly followed with their cases. Both puffed softly as they climbed the stairs.

CHAPTER 5

After a sleepless night, Amanda dragged herself out of bed. When she'd called Pauline, after the twins were settled in last night, she got no response. Pauline had already left for the airport. Torn between going to London and staying, she showered, dressed, then sat at the kitchen table sipping hot coffee and considering her options.

How should she tell the aunts about the recent change of circumstances? Keep it cool, she thought. I'll say something like, "He found a sweeter chocolate chip cookie." She paused. "Maybe he's out chasing his youth, found a teenager to adore." Of course that wasn't necessarily true. She found herself smiling. His new girlfriend might actually be in her twenties, or maybe thirties, but certainly not any older.

She ran several possibilities through her mind, finished her coffee, and then looked out the bay window. Molly and Hallie were in the garden, pulling weeds she'd let go to seed. The compost pile beside the garden shed had grown almost a foot since the last time she looked at it. Damn, she thought, why did they get up so early?

Molly saw her and waved, then motioned to her sister, and they started for the house. Molly wore striped overalls several sizes too big, with a blue cotton shirt. Hallie wore cut-off overalls and a tee shirt of olive green. As they approached the house, both took long strides. They would be considered plain, Amanda thought. But when they smiled, their eyes danced with merriment, a hint of mischief gleaming in them. She liked these women.

"You've such an awful lot to do with this big house and garden. Thought we'd give you a hand," Hallie said, as they entered the kitchen. She took off gloves and dropped them to a chair. "We found these in the garden shed. Hope you don't mind us using them."

Amanda shook her head and smiled. "Not at all."

"Such a gorgeous place here," Molly said. "No wonder Preston bragged about the garden in his letters."

"Oh, did he?" Amanda replied with disgust. "He considered the garden my domain. He seldom worked out there." She paused. "What would you like for breakfast?" She intended to be cheerful today for the sake of her two guests, but she hoped they'd want dry cereal. She'd had no interest in cooking since Preston left.

"We always have eggs, bacon, toast and oatmeal," Hallie said. "Of course, that keeps us going until supper."

"We can't continue eating that way," Molly cut in. "We'd soon be blimps." She laughed at her own words. "Do you have eggs?" When Amanda nodded, she said, "Show me the skillet. Hallie, you make the toast and Amanda can set the table."

Amazed, Amanda watched the two open and close cupboards and drawers, until they found what they needed for their culinary tasks. For the first time in weeks, Amanda found herself chuckling and feeling light-hearted.

Preston once told her that his aunts worked in their father's feed store, and then inherited it. Both were husky and obviously very capable.

They all ate heartily, Amanda enjoying the food. After breakfast, she said, "I'll give you a tour of the area, if you like. Show you about."

Hallie turned to Molly. "You're the oldest. You take charge."

"Of what?" Amanda asked.

Molly gave a reticent smile. "Then you clear up here, while Amanda and I have a talk on the window seat." She nodded to it, stood, then took Amanda's hand and pulled her toward the cushioned seats. When they were seated, Molly studied Amanda's face for several moments.

At a loss for words, Amanda couldn't think what Molly intended to say. The women had become sober-faced, no merriment in their eyes now. "What is it?" she asked.

"I won't beat about the bush," Molly said. "It's about Preston." When Amanda gasped, she said, "No, no, I'm sure he's fine, if that's what you're thinking. It's just that we know what he's done."

"How could you?"

"Let me start at the beginning." Molly said. "About a month or so ago we sold our store, intending to move out this way. Always promised Preston we'd retire out here. We were going to take a little vacation first, but then this call came from Pauline. Didn't know what to do, then. We canceled the trip. As our apartment was above the store, we didn't have to sell a house. The only thing we could think to do was come here and help you."

Puzzled, Amanda stared at her. "Did you know Pauline intended to go to New York, too?"

From in front of the sink, Hallie piped up, "That's why we didn't come until last night. Wanted to avoid her as much a possible. Strange creature, that. In the area of brains, she's a quart short."

"Don't pass on your dislikes," Molly cautioned.

"Not just dislikes, facts, too." Hallie returned. "Anyway, get on with the story." She turned back to the sink.

"Why do you feel I need help?" Amanda said. "I'm fine, as you can see."

"Not so," Molly corrected. "Garden's full of weeds. Heaven knows what else needs help." She placed a large hand on Amanda's shoulder. "You see, Pauline called especially to tell us about Preston. Everything."

Stunned, Amanda frowned. "What do you mean by that?"

"Preston walked out on you." Molly pushed her bangs aside as if uneasy with the conversation.

"Pauline told you that?" She wanted to give Pauline a swift kick. "When?"

Molly considered her reply for several moments. "The day before it happened."

Then Hallie cut in. "I'd like to give that boy a trip to the wood shed. Completely lost his senses."

"Now Hallie," Molly scolded again. "Who's telling this anyway? Take care of those dishes, and leave Amanda to me."

Amanda didn't relish being left to anyone. She stood and stared down at Molly. "You're telling me all of you knew about this? I had to call Preston's office to learn where he had gone, and I've only just been able to pry the address out of his partner." Tears of anger stung her eyes, but she managed to blink them back. "Why wasn't I told?"

"We hadn't met you," Molly defended, anguish creasing her brow. "How would you have felt to get such a call from strangers?"

The table had been cleared, and Amanda sat at it, her arms folded on the top and her head resting on them. Humiliation filled her. Why had Preston done this? Trying to understand his actions, she felt a new sobering realization. Preston had never loved her as deeply as she had loved him. Slowly she raised her head. "Do you also know the name of the new love?"

A look of surprised flashed over Molly's face. "Don't you know?"

"I've no idea."

Molly looked over at Hallie and shook her head ever so slightly, then said, "Well, we can't help you there. Probably someone who tickled his fancy."

"That's not all she tickled," Hallie cut in as she turned to face them. The dishes were now in the dishwasher.

"To get on with it," Molly said. "We knew from Preston's letters that you were never at fault. So...we want to help you, take care of the garden and house, until we find a place of our own."

Still stunned, Amanda replied, "You're welcome to stay here as long as you like." She wanted to tell them of her planned trip to London, but that could wait.

"Have you heard from Preston?" Hallie asked, as she joined Amanda at the table.

"Hallie," Molly scolded. "That's none of your business."

"Since you know all about it anyway, I don't mind. He hasn't called or written."

"What about finances? Has he left you well enough off? If not, we can help you. Got a good price for our place."

Amanda hadn't considered this before, but knew she should have. Had he left her anything at all? She'd have to check into it tomorrow, but grew cold with anxiety, almost hating to find out.

"I'd like to wring his neck," Hallie said. "Don't believe in divorce, not when the man is having a mid-life crisis. Brainless twit."

Molly shook her head, as if hearing too much lip from a sassy child. "That's enough of that."

"You're not the CEO any longer," Hallie shot back. "Can't tell me what to say or think."

"Well, just keep it to yourself. Don't upset Amanda any further."

"I'm fine," Amanda said. "But like Hallie, I'd like to wring Preston's neck, too."

"There you go," Hallie laughed. "Two of us ought to do a half-way decent job of it, if we can catch him."

This seemed like the appropriate time to speak of her proposed trip to London. She told them and waited for their reaction.

"Is that such a good idea?" Molly asked.

"Let her do it," Hallie said. "Get things settled."

Ridges of disapproval formed on Molly's brow. "No need to seek after more misery. She's had enough of that already."

Amanda looked from one to the other, certain they both knew more than they were telling.

"She'll find out in the end," Hallie defended. She pushed her hair behind her left ear, as if making hearing easier, but it was too short to stay put.

Molly shook her head. "Maybe, but later is better than sooner in this case." She turned to Amanda. "The other party isn't totally to blame, you know. Preston is also an idiot."

"Damned fool," Hallie muttered. "Worse than witless. An ass. Shook off a feed bag filled with oats so he could get at one filled with Tansy. Now I ask you, what kind of sense does..."

"It don't," Molly cut in. "None of it does, but Amanda better think twice before she goes off hunting him."

"I have," Amanda replied. "Over and over again. Who is this woman? It keeps churning about in my mind. Do I know her?"

"Take my word for it," Hallie said, her voice ringing with distaste. "She's no one you'd want to know, if you had the choice." She paused to think. "On second thought maybe Molly is right about not going."

"I am. You're unhappy now, but the tables will turn, you know. Preston won't be happy long, if he is now. You can bet on that."

"Not with this new lollypop," Hallie added. "He's bound to be miserable about now, and guilty as hell."

Milo waited for Amanda to answer the phone, tapping his foot impatiently. When she answered, he said, "I need some advice from Preston." He'd called every week since Jackie had left, surely he was home now.

"I'm sorry, Dad. He's not back from London," Amanda responded.

"What? What's so damned important in London that he has to stay all this time?"

"Business," she replied. "He's away on business."

"Can't be keeping him this long."

"Can I help you?" she asked.

"I doubt it, but give it a try anyway. Jackie finally called from Paris. Get this. Four weeks late. Can you imagine? I'd called all over Paris trying to get in touch with her. Says she was terribly busy. Too busy to call me, her husband. I told her what I thought, by George."

"What's the problem?"

He resented her lack of concern. "The problem is her request. That's what the problem is."

"What request?" She now sounded short-tempered.

"What the hell's the matter with you? What have you got to be snippy about? Never had a problem in your whole life. Spoiled, that's it. Jackie spoiled you."

For several moments Amanda didn't respond. Finally, she said, "So? What's your problem?"

"She wants me to send her the harp, that's what!" Now his voice rang with disgust, and he didn't care.

"Are you going to?"

"Hell no! Ruin it to ship it all that way. What does she want it for, anyway?"

"Didn't you ask her?"

"What kind of fool do you take me for? Of course I asked her." He wondered why his daughter seemed so dull-witted today.

"What's the harm in sending it?"

"Ruin it, as I said. It cost me several thousand dollars, you know."

"Do you need to sell it to pay your bills?"

"You know better than that."

"Then send it. It's hers, isn't it?"

"That's not the point."

"Then what is the point?"

He thought a moment, trying to make up his mind whether to mention his worries. But whom could he tell if not his daughter? "What if she intends to leave me? If I keep the harp, she'll have to come home for it."

"Did she say that's what she's doing?"

"I'm sure I heard it in her voice."

Amanda remained silent for a long time. He thought she had left the phone. Then she said, "You can't tie her to the bed, Dad. If she's going to leave you, she'll do it even without the harp."

"I don't think so," he replied, not at all convinced. "She loves that harp."

"Not as much as she loves to travel without you."

He bristled, but remained silent.

"Look, Dad," Amanda said, her voice more kindly. "If Jackie wants to leave you, she will. Why give her an excuse by being stingy about letting her have her own harp? Send it to her with your love."

After some thought, he replied, "Hell, I think maybe you're right. I'll do just that."

After he hung up, he decided to sweeten the offer with a good-sized check, and a love letter. He hadn't told her how much he loved her for a long time. As he sat thinking, Agatha came into the room.

"Like a glass of cold lemonade?" she asked, setting it on the table beside him. Her graying hair, pulled back in a bun, was damp from recent washing.

"Great," he replied. Then thinking of Jackie again, he said, "I'll get my angel home soon, Agatha, one way or another. Even if I have to go and get her."

Agatha gave him a strange look, shook her head and left. Milo couldn't begin to read it, but he'd always known Agatha never respected Jackie. Jackie, the love of his life. Yes, she'd come home to him, and soon.

CHAPTER 6

Preston had left the hotel angry at himself and Jackie. He only had been in the office ten minutes when Jackie called. They had quarreled over her contact with Milo. She'd neglected to tell Milo she wanted a divorce. She'd gone to Paris, called Milo, and pretended to be living at a hotel there, all to convince Milo to ship her the harp.

While she was away, Preston had slept without the pangs of guilt disturbing his sleep. But this morning Jackie carried on about searching for a permanent home. She wanted a cottage outside of London, but close enough to catch a train in two or three times a week. She'd never before liked living in the country, and Preston couldn't understand why she wanted to now.

The first thing she said, when he picked up the phone was, "Can you come home early?"

Her bubbling voice no longer thrilled him, instead, it sent shivers of discontent chasing over him. "What's up?" he asked, bracing for another argument.

"A cottage. Down in Kent. Less than a half-hour train ride. I just talked to the agent. He said it would sell fast. We'd have to move on it right away, if we want it. He'll meet us in Petts Woods station at two."

Preston closed his eyes a moment in speechless dread. "That's why you want me to come home early?"

"If you get back here at one, we'd have plenty of time to take a good look at it. It sounds like a wonderful cottage," she said.

"What kind of cottage?" he asked, hoping to deter her. "How old? Does it have plumbing? Electricity?" He thought some of the older ones hadn't been modernized.

"Of course," she shot back, "I wouldn't have anything that wasn't up-to-date. What kind of question was that?"

Now he took another tack. "I can't leave before four." He could, but wouldn't. It seemed strange to be always thinking up excuses, lying so frequently. It made him uncomfortable. That first lie to Amanda had started it, along with the new knack for being evasive. The more he practiced, the easier it seemed, though it left an acrid taste in his mouth.

After a long silence, she snapped, "Then I'll just have to go alone, won't I?" Angrily, she added, "And I may well be late getting back." She hung up.

He ran his hand over his chin, contemplating what to do. Why should he go, when he didn't want to? She couldn't do anything about buying a cottage without him. No, the expense of the place right now set his nerves on edge. And cottages were priced high, out of range for most buyers. Jackie had no sense of values, no sense of obligations, no sense of... loyalty. He hated to think it, but he knew that deep down his own values had slipped beyond recognition.

If Jackie's love for him couldn't withstand living in a flat, then what was it worth? He swiveled his chair and stood to look out the window. The mid-June sun shone brightly.

Pigeons filled the air around and over the building tops. He couldn't see it, but Trafalgar Square lay only a few blocks away. Watching the bird's flight, he envied their dignified freedom. With Amanda, he'd had such freedom, had reveled in it, savored it. Not now. Not with this woman who dominated his life, leaving him very few moments for himself, wanting to know his every thought. No time to read, think, or even wallow in misery. That's what it had become. Jackie smothered him. Her wild embraces, that had seemed so wonderful at first, had become tiresome every time he returned from the office. And the constant love-making. "Oh, Amanda. I was such a fool," he muttered.

No, he determined, I won't buy a cottage or anything else. We'll rent a flat, or stay right where we are. Living in London had lost its sheen, and living with Jackie had become a noose. A large lump formed in his throat. He swallowed, then took a deep, rueful breath and went back to his desk. If Jackie arrived home late, he'd have a few moments to himself. What a relief! Maybe she'd stay away for a day or two.

Pauline hurried to catch her flight back to Seattle. A redcap carried her extra luggage, while she carried only the one she'd take on board with her. But many other packages were being shipped by UPS. The weather was hot and muggy. She'd known better than to wear the outfit she had on, but she wanted to be seen in it when she arrived home. The red blouse, under the black leather jacket, now stuck to her body like wet paper, but she wouldn't take off the jacket until she boarded the plane. And the short black leather skirt felt like a hot, wet towel around her waist and hips. A few people seemed to be watching her. She reveled in it.

I'll be the envy of every woman in Seattle. I'll make waves, she told herself. I haven't before because of Preston and Amanda. They are the cause of my problems, always cautioning me not to make a fool of myself. Ha ha- I'll show them.

When she finally found her seat and took off her jacket, she breathed a sigh of relief, moving her shoulders in circles to relieve the aching neck. She twisted it from side to side, then her head back and forth. Finally, she relaxed against the seat. She'd had a wonderful time buying designer clothes. She had, in fact, purchased a suit by Richard Tyler, boots by Gucci, a waffle-weave cashmere top, a lace evening dress, and... She couldn't remember them all. But they were all designer clothes, and very smart.

She intended to travel to Paris in the fall for spring clothing. Then in the spring she'd do it all over again for winter clothes. What a wonderful life to be completely free of constraints from Preston, who always seemed too ready to give unwanted advice, and never gave her credit for knowing anything. Well, she'd show him and everyone else, especially Cole. He'd come to see how independent she was, not a clinging vine at all. But smart, oh so smart- looking.

As she sat thinking, she smiled to herself. Wouldn't that mousy, soon-to-be-ex-sister-in-law be jealous with envy over the clothes. She could hardly wait to see Amanda's face. Amanda, who always got everything she wanted.

Her own new image, closely cropped hair, mannishly styled, and her wonderful wardrobe, would stun her friends. And Cole? He'd be as shaken as the others would. She tipped the seat back and closed her eyes, imagining the eventual results of her new image. She would plan a wedding, one that would most certainly live up to her expectations, a lavish wedding. Her friends could help her plan it. Then she wondered how long it would take her to get Cole to propose? She'd made Jackie's dreams come true, hadn't she? Well, she most certainly could do the same for herself, then leave Cole at the altar, stunned and anguished.

No one met her at the airport, which upset her, though she'd never notified anyone of her arrival. Still, all of them would see her soon enough, envy her, and admire her.

Amanda and the twins had just returned from a sight-seeing trip around the area. They had driven into Seattle and around the housing areas Amanda had thought they might like, then back to Kent. Hallie had become intrigued with the big city, Molly with the pastoral scenes around Kent. All were now in the kitchen.

"Just think of all the things we could do in Seattle," Hallie purred. "Movies, arts, concerts, all at our doorstep. I could find myself in Seattle."

"You're not lost," Molly scolded. "Anyway, I can't see the pair of us trotting off to a concert in striped overalls. We don't own any fancy clothes."

With a snort, Hallie replied, "What's the matter with buying some? We can afford it." Her chin shot up in determination. "We aren't destitute, you know. Not by a long shot."

"We'd have to have them specially made. That's expensive," Molly replied.

"So, why not ready-made clothes? Aren't they good enough for you?" Hallie asked. She looked at Amanda, made a face and groaned.

"Oh, sure," Molly replied. "That's not the point. We've got muscles where most women don't have them. Arms don't fit the sleeves. Remember when we bought those women's wash and dry blouses?" She looked at Hallie with an expression of disbelief.

Hallie laughed loudly. "I sure do. Split mine the first time I hefted a sack of chicken feed."

"And they didn't make good rags, either. Couldn't wring any water out of 'em," Molly said, turning to Amanda. "Mostly, we've bought men's shirts and overalls. Easier to work in, especially the kind of work we did."

"Well, it's about time we started to dress like women." Then turning to Amanda, Hallie added, "The fellows got so they treated us like one of them. Got so they never offered to carry out their own sacks of feed. Lazy cusses." She plopped to a chair by the table.

Amanda slipped off her shoes and sat at the kitchen table, too. She'd thoroughly enjoyed the day. The two aunts were always laughing and joking about something. "Why did neither of you marry?" she asked. "You'd both have made wonderful mothers."

Both women broke into laughter again, then Hallie said, "Never could find a man willing to take on both of us."

Amanda didn't understand. "What?"

"How else could we stay together? When we were young, we vowed never to be separated, if we couldn't find a man big enough to handle...."

Molly cut in, "The only man I took a shine to moved to Tennessee. I'd never live there, not in a million years. And she," she nodded toward Hallie, "got sweet on a man only half her size. I couldn't go for that."

"Couldn't always be picking him up to kiss him," Hallie said, grinning broadly. "Not good for a man's ego." Then after a moment's thought, she added, "Anyway, he was enamored of the business more un me."

Soberly, Molly said, "We're not what you'd call feminine women. They used to call the likes of us tomboys, and we never grew out of it. And who wants to marry one of them?"

"That's only the half of it," Hallie added, "We were pretty choosy in our younger days. But we've had a good life, haven't we, Molly? No complaints from us."

Molly stretched as if ready for an afternoon's nap, then she said, "Let's give Amanda a break, twin. Time to herself. We've been chewing on her ears most of the day. We really haven't unpacked yet." She turned and said, "Come on twin, let's get out of her hair for a while." With that, they picked up their ample shoulder bags and trotted off, prattling as they went.

Relieved to have a few moments to herself, Amanda found a shady spot in the back yard and lay on her back, knees bent and her bare feet shoved into the cool grass. She'd mowed the lawn less than a week ago, but it needed cutting again. So much for telling Cole she wouldn't look after the yard, though she'd not originally intended to. He probably knew she couldn't let it go, not after how hard she'd worked to keep it groomed. At least she'd have help with it now. Why, already the weeds had been pulled and stacked on the compost pile, thanks to her guests.

More and more she found herself adjusting to the prospect of living without Preston. Brooke had worked out a very good life for herself as a single woman. So can I, she thought. I simply have to put my mind to it.

She thought of Jackie in Paris. She'd been away much longer than usual, and now wanting her harp? How long did she intend to stay away? Had she taken another lover? Strange way to do things. Perhaps she'd soon tire of him and come home. She always did.

Amanda turned on her side to look at the brick patio. Clover had begun to grow in between the bricks, and she vowed to get out the weed killer and take care of it tomorrow. "No more mooning around, and Molly and Hallie will see that I don't." She chuckled to herself.

She'd inquired at the bank about her account. Preston had deposited a great deal of money before he left her. She'd have no financial worries, until she could get her college degree. Then she'd really be on her own. She thought of her options. Stay in Kent, or move into Seattle. Perhaps even move to Portland. But she had plenty of time to decide. Two things she needed to do soon? Make arrangement for fall term classes at the university, then take that trip to London.

CHAPTER 7

Preston refused to look at the cottage Jackie had insisted on owning. Furious, she'd threatened to go home, but Preston couldn't be badgered into it. She finally relented, still hoping to somehow persuade him she needed a place in the country.

However, the real reason she kept from him. As part of an earlier arrangement, when Milo discovered her with a lover, she agreed she would never again stray. If she did, she would forfeit any claim to Milo's property. So Milo must never find out about Preston, at least not until she had the divorce papers in her hands, and the settlement check in the bank. She imagined living in the country would make it harder for Milo to locate her, if he tried to track her down.

But today she wouldn't think about it. She'd do some shopping to lighten her mood, perhaps use her credit cards. She roamed around the shops on Regent Street, Bond and New Bond, but her mind wasn't on clothes, nor could she force it that direction. If only she could play her harp, raise her spirits to a higher, more gratifying realm. Catch the vibrations of heaven, which she often felt while playing.

In desperation, she hunted for a music store, hailing a cab and telling him what she wanted. As a child, whenever she didn't want to practice, her mother always said, “God loves music, Jackie, especially harp music. That’s your way into his good graces. Concentrate on the big things, then God will forgive the little mistakes.” Jackie now deeply believed those words.

Within minutes she was inside the shop, admiring a 38 string Eclipse Harp.

A salesman asked, “May I help you?” He wore a Groucho Marx mustache, and a never-ending smile beneath it.

Jackie looked at him with soulful eyes. “I’m thinking about replacing my harp. May I try this one, to be sure it’s what I want?”

“Most certainly,” he beamed. He immediately provided her with a stool.

She sat down, running her fingers in a glissando over the strings. Then she began to play Ave Maria, a piece she knew God loved. Quickly lost in deep reverie, she didn’t notice customers forming a circle around her, listening quietly. She played with a sense of deep devotion to the instrument and music. Her emotions soared to a height she hadn’t experienced for several weeks, not since leaving Seattle. She reveled in it, playing the piece over again.

In a state of euphoria, she finished playing, got up and walked to the door, never hearing the applause that followed her. Yes, she had to have a harp, and soon.

When the door closed behind her, tears streamed down her cheeks. To her, playing the harp seemed like performing devotions, supplicating God for forgiveness of her transgressions. And she recognized many misdeeds over the years, but they were surely appeased by her playing. Milo had never understood that. She hoped Preston would. She’d played with the Seattle symphony for years, and hated to give that up, though she’d given up other groups. To compensate, she’d played extensively at home. Right now she needed that harp, her music, her pathway to God. She’d go back to the hotel, tell her volumes of diary all about it. She was glad she’d burned the whole lot back home. Didn’t want Milo to ever read them.

The twins had been with Amanda two weeks, and London was again on her mind. All three had been working in the garden, but now they sat relaxing on the patio. The twins sat on lawn chairs, Amanda on the grass beside them.

"I'll be going to London soon," Amanda said. She watched Molly's face for any trace of disapproval. "Just for a few days, to get some things straightened out with Preston."

"Are you sure you should?" Molly asked. She unbuttoned the top two buttons of her plaid shirt and fanned herself with a large hand.

"Yes, I'm sure. This is something I've got to do. I can't get it off my mind." She rolled over and stretched out on the cool grass.

"Just know you might get hurt even more. But as far as this place is concerned, we'll look after it," Molly said.

"I appreciate that. I'll make arrangements tomorrow."

Hallie spoke up. "I'll go with you, if you need company." Her face beamed with anticipation.

"I have to go alone," Amanda apologized, regretting the need to hurt any feelings. "I might not even stay more than a day or two."

"Why would she need help from you?" Molly asked, turning to her sister, who sat limply in cut-off overalls, and a short-sleeved blouse. Her well-developed muscles rippled when she moved her arms.

Indignant, Hallie raised her chin. "Because she might need support, that's all."

"I don't suppose you'd be anything but in the way," Molly said, with a laugh.

Hallie shrugged. "I'm not like you. I want to see some of the world before I die."

"This isn't the time to see the world, or die," Molly countered.

"As far as you're concerned, there never is a time to travel."

"Don't be a baby," Molly chided. "We'll do some traveling as soon as we get settled here."

Hallie looked at her sister, scowling as she pulled on her overall strap, then shortened it. "Oh, sure. When the cows come home."

Molly laughed. "We'll be on our way quicker, if you'll settle on living around here some place."

"I could always move into Seattle," Hallie threatened. "Live alone. I don't have to live with you."

"You could, but you won't," Molly replied.

Amanda, not certain whether the argument was serious, said, "You could always live in an apartment, before you buy a place. See if you like Seattle. That way you'd be sure before you put out much money."

"Money's not the problem," Hallie replied. She jabbed her thumb in the direction of Molly. "She still thinks she's the boss."

Molly looked out over the lawn at the bower on the back fence and yawned lazily, ignoring her sister.

"All because she was born first," Hallie muttered. "Oh, well" she added with a sigh. "She got the brains, but I got the classic good looks. A regular goddess."

All three laughed, Hallie laughing the loudest.

"We've had this same argument millions of times," Molly said. "Always turns out the same way."

"I buckle under," Hallie admitted. "But only because she's ten pounds heavier than me."

"Bigger brains," Molly bragged, then yawned again.

"Bigger ego," Hallie corrected, slouching lower on the chair.

Turning her attention to Amanda, Molly asked, "When do you intend to go to London?"

"As soon as I can get a seat."

"Will you let Preston know you're coming?"

"No way," Amanda replied, sitting up to look at Molly. "The idea is to surprise him."

"And perhaps yourself."

"So be it." Amanda had no idea what would happen upon seeing Preston again, and she refused to speculate. It made no difference who the other woman might be. The end result would be the same. A divorce. A prospect she would never have considered just a few months ago. However, she did wonder how Preston was reacting to his abrupt desertion of her. He had a conscience that pricked over the slightest transgressions, and he certainly would feel guilty over what he'd done.

Let him fry, she thought, and the woman, too. If I had a good match, I'd help them strike the fire. Then after a moment, she relented. Perhaps the woman is someone she might like, under different circumstances. But she'd know soon enough.

"You're frowning," Hallie said. "Having second thoughts about going?"

"No." Amanda's mind went back to Preston and the woman. Had he known her in Seattle? Had they both moved away to avoid a scandal?

This new thought disturbed her. "I've got to go right away, though. Get it off my mind."

Before Amanda went to bed, she stood before the mirror to study herself, wondering why Preston had left her. As I'm a blonde, has he chosen a brunette or a redhead? Is she the opposite of me, heavy, smarter, less accommodating? She stewed about it in bed. Sleep finally came, but no answers formed in her mind.

After dinner the next day, as Amanda sat making a list of questions for Preston, Brooke called. "Haven't gone to London yet?"

"No. Preston's aunts arrived just after I saw you. But I'm going to make arrangements tomorrow." The twins were at the kitchen table studying a local map.

"Don't, Amanda," Brooke cautioned.

"Why?" She'd already had this conversation with Brooke, but remained determined.

"Best advice I can give you. Just file for divorce. Let him keep whatever dignity he has left. You'll be able to get a better settlement that way. He won't fight it so much."

"I don't care about his dignity."

"You might make things worse."

"I don't see how."

After a pause, Brooke said, "Have you seen an attorney yet?"

"When I come back, I will."

"You're doing it the wrong way around." After a pause, she added, "Anyway, I didn't call for that reason. I want to tell you I just learned about three sisters who need a home. I've opted to try and get them."

"Wonderful. When will you know?" Amanda thought the decision a fast one, considering the recent intention of redecorating the house first.

"Not for a few weeks, at best. But I'm excited. They're just 3, 5 and 6 years old.

Puzzled, Amanda said, "How can you handle them and still work?"

"I found a woman who needs the work and a place to live. She's agreed to live in and look after them. Isn't that great?"

"Wow, you work fast." For a brief moment, Amanda felt pangs of jealousy, but immediately swallowed them. "It's really wonderful, I envy you."

"Good. Then maybe you'll become a doting aunt. They have no relatives, but still need birthday presents and Christmas and the lot. You know. Emotional support from relatives."

"I'd love to. Of course I will."

"Then call me as soon as you get back. I'll need all kinds of support myself."

After having played the harp in a shop, Jackie sank into a depression, which Preston viewed as a childish sulk. No matter how he'd tried to cajole her, Jackie would not relent. Finally, he said, "I've got tickets for the ballet at Covent Garden tonight. If you won't come with me, I'll take my secretary, or go alone."

He hadn't wanted to see the ballet, but knew she did, so bought the tickets two weeks ago as a surprise.

"You wouldn't," she gasped. "Take another woman out while I'm here with you? Cheat on me?" She swelled with indignation.

He stared at her, not believing her sense of reasoning. Hadn't both of them done exactly that? "Why not? We're used to doing such things." Suddenly he hoped she'd still refuse, then he'd go somewhere alone, but not to the ballet. Perhaps go to a pub, or a walk down Regent Street, then to Picadilly Circus. Anyplace but the rooms here at the Savoy. Tourists were always walking the streets, why not him?

He couldn't remember the last time he'd sat on any cool grass, and suddenly he wanted to. He'd go to Hyde Park on the way home. Sit until he couldn't delay going back any longer. He hoped Jackie would be asleep by then.

"What we did before has nothing to do with now," Jackie finally said, a deep resentment in her voice. "We're staying in," she added. "To get a few things settled."

He looked at her, puzzled, and couldn't remember what the conversation had been about. He knew what her order meant. She'd try to browbeat him into compliance, whatever that might be. He knew the scenario by heart. Anger, frustration, tears. Then the "poor me" routine, as if he'd ill-treated her. How come he'd never seen all this before? Never even imagined it.

Jackie kept talking, but deep in his own thoughts, Preston ignored the grunts and whines, grabbed his jacket from the closet and headed for the door. Jackie began screaming at him as the door slammed. Poor Milo, he thought. How has he put up with this all these years? God! What a life. What a sucker! But with his next breath, he realized Milo wasn't the sucker. No one pushed Milo around. Maybe that's what attracted Jackie to him. He considered himself to be easy-going, amiable, an easy target for someone like Jackie.

As he waited for the elevator, he realized he couldn't take much more. But when should he tell her? Perhaps in a few days, when he'd worked out in his mind exactly what he wanted to say and do. At this point, he couldn't even recall what had attracted him to Jackie in the first place.

His thoughts turned to Amanda. How he wanted to see her, talk to her, feel her gentle presence as he sat reading by the fireplace, and smoking his pipe. His pipe now had a bitter taste. He seldom smoked. The mental picture made the back of his eyes sting. "Amanda, what a fool I've been," he muttered softly, as if Jackie might overhear him.

CHAPTER 8

Not until after she was seated on the plane did Amanda begin to worry about confronting Preston. And she had a full twelve hours to worry. She kept mulling over Brooke's advice, and then Molly's cautions. Did either of them know or suspect what kind of greeting awaited her? Of course not. How could they? Unless Pauline knew who the other woman was, and told the twins.

She watched the movie to take her mind off her worries. When it finally finished, she had no idea what it was about, or its title. Her thoughts could not be swayed from Preston.

She knew he stayed at the Savoy Hotel, so she had booked a room at the Berkshire, close enough to walk, she thought. Perhaps she'd sit in the Savoy lobby and watch, see if Preston came in with his...whatever she was. She dismissed the thought immediately. Suddenly she didn't want to see the other woman. Didn't want to know her identity. See Preston and get out of there, she admonished herself.

Amanda assumed he kept the same working hours as he kept in Seattle. Perhaps she'd wait until he got home from work, then walk over and confront him. But what brought her this far? Stubbornness, she realized. She should have hired a lawyer, let him talk to Preston, make all the arrangements. Then why hadn't she done so? Brooke had suggested just that. I should have done it, she thought ruefully, her unexpected nervousness mounting.

Pauline had been back from New York for a few days, and no one had called her about the trip. She felt slighted, with her closet full of new clothes, her hairstyle changed, and no one to admire them. And she couldn't stop yearning for Cole, though she wouldn't have him now.

When she could stand it no longer, she dialed Amanda. A strange voice answered. "Who is this? she demanded

"Molly Leigh."

Gasping, Pauline said, "What in the world are you doing there?"

"Visiting Amanda," she replied. "So, you're back from New York." Not an ounce of curiosity showed in her voice. In fact, Molly sounded completely uninterested in Pauline's affairs.

"Let me talk to Amanda," Pauline said in a thin and cutting voice.

"Can't. She isn't here right now."

"Then where is she?"

After a moment, Molly replied, "Took a small vacation. How was yours? Get all the clothes you went after?"

Pleased to be asked, she replied, "Yes. Designer clothes. Gorgeous clothes. You must come over and admire them. They cost me thousands." That ought to impress her, she thought, the old hag.

"Didn't spend all your money in one place, I hope."

"Oh, I didn't, but I'm going to Paris later. To get my spring wardrobe." She paused, giving Molly a chance to take it all in. She'd never liked her twin aunts. Too mannish, too dull. And they always spoke their minds without considering her feelings. But she knew she'd better be careful, lest Preston find out. They'd no doubt tell him lies about her. Then she'd be in for a taste of his wrath. "How are you and Aunt Hallie since you retired?"

"We're doing just fine. Enjoying our stay. In fact we're looking for a house. We intend to live in this area. Always promised Preston we would."

The new information stunned Pauline, she couldn't think for a moment, then she said, "But he doesn't live here any more. I told you that.

He lives in London. Anyway, I doubt you'll like the area. Rains all the time, then fog when the rain quits."

Molly laughed. "Just what we need for our delicate complexions. I'll be glad to see the rains start."

"You won't be, once they really get going," she returned. She wondered if she could say anything to discourage Molly's enthusiasm. Then she thought of Amanda again. "Where did you say Amanda has gone?"

"I didn't. She just took a few days off."

Pauline began to worry that Amanda had gone to London. Would she be that stupid? "Did she go by plane?" she asked.

"For a short vacation?" Molly sounded amused.

"I just wondered. She didn't go to London, did she?"

Molly laughed loudly. "Now why would she go there for a short vacation?"

Relieved, Pauline said, "Oh, I just wondered. But it was certainly rude for her to take a vacation with you visiting her."

"Not so. We came unannounced. Perhaps we should move over to your place 'til she gets back. I'm sure you'd love to cook for us."

"I don't cook," Pauline snapped. "Anyway, Amanda has more room than I do."

"Well, I'm glad you had such a good time in New York. Come see us, if you have the time. Good-bye." She hung up without further comment.

"How dare you treat me that way?" Pauline shouted into the phone. "You've no right to dismiss me. You'll come to regret that." She slammed down the receiver and paced about. After a few moments, she told herself, "Don't let that old hag sidetrack your goals. Think about Cole."

She remembered him saying she stuck to him like glue, on that one date with him. You just wait and see, Cole, she thought. I'll be so popular you'll have to fight your way to me. Make me notice you. Beg me to marry you. She laughed triumphantly, a strange, wicked laugh.

But she couldn't just walk into his office to show off. It would have to be a casual meeting, one where she could feign indifference to his presence. Pretend to hardly notice him. But how?

Amanda had reason to see Cole. She'd tag along as if shopping with Amanda. He'd soon see how she'd changed, how desirable she'd become.

"Clothes make the woman," she chortled to herself. "A woman you'll chase after, Cole."

In front of the hall mirror, she watched an unfamiliar woman staring back at her, a very smartly dressed woman with brown hair cut short and sleeked back in a the latest style. She wore blue eye shadow, and her eyebrows were plucked to a pencil thin line. She shivered with the anticipated pleasure of seeing her friends admire her, congratulate her.

Pauline still had a hard time recognizing her own reflection. But she'd get used to it, just as everyone else would. Especially Cole. "You're on your way," she told the reflection. "Without Preston to interfere, it should be a snap."

"But I've got to have a harp," Jackie was telling Preston. They'd been arguing all evening, and she didn't seem to be able to wear him down. Frustration filled her, almost to her limits now. She couldn't charge a harp on her credit cards. Milo had the bank cut the limit she could charge some time ago.

"Then call Milo. Tell him the truth."

"You know I can't do that. Surely you understand?"

He shook his head. "I'm afraid I don't. I'm beginning to think there's little about you I do understand." He put aside his pipe, now hating the taste. He stood, then walked to the window. "We've made a terrible mistake, you and I."

She rushed to his side. "Oh, Preston, don't even think that. We're made for each other. We've known it all along." She slipped her arms around his neck. "Darling, kiss me." She pulled his head to where she could kiss his mouth, but he didn't respond. She stepped back, not understanding his mood. "What's wrong? All I did was say I needed a harp. They aren't that expensive."

He turned his back to her. "It isn't the harp. It's the deceit. It's choking me." He spun around to face her, as she began to cry.

"Oh, Preston," she sobbed. "I love you so much more than I've ever loved anyone before." She covered her face with her hands. "I hate it when...we have times like this. Not...not understanding each other's needs."

"Have we ever?" His careless reply tore at her heart.

"You know we have." Her legs began to tremble, and she grabbed the back of a chair to steady herself. "Don't you love me anymore?" When he didn't reply, she demanded, "I suppose you hate me now."

"Of course not."

When he gave no further assurance of his love, she began to sob loudly. After several minutes, she controlled her emotions. "This is what happens...when we're too cramped. We need a house, Preston. Can't you see that, darling?"

"I recognize more serious problems, Jackie. Ones we have to resolve. We need an understanding soon."

She rushed from the room, crying out, "All this because...I want a harp." She stopped in the doorway of the bedroom. "I've given up everything for you. You might at least see that I have a harp to entertain myself when you're at work."

"It isn't the harp, Jackie. It's you and me."

"No, it's not. You've become as money-pinching as Milo."

She slammed the door behind her and sat on the floor, her back to it. After a few moments, her eyes were dry, and she began to smile. Of course, Preston needed a vacation. He's worked too hard. A vacation would sweeten him up. Then he'll want my forgiveness. Yes, we'll take a vacation in Paris. Smiling broadly, she stood, anxious to start packing.

CHAPTER 9

Every time Preston tried to reason with Jackie, she changed the subject, remembered an appointment, or found an excuse to hurriedly leave the hotel. He'd given up on renting a flat, and the expense of the hotel was bothering him, cutting too deeply into his funds. He'd prefer to talk to Jackie about separating, but all she could think of was that vacation in France. As things were, he knew he'd simply have to make the decision himself, and return to Seattle alone. Jackie could do as she pleased. The turbulence in his mind made it impossible for him to any longer make business decisions, and he couldn't continue like this any more.

Jackie had just left the apartment in a rush to buy shampoo. It had rained during the day, and puffy clouds still scurried across the sky. Preston shrugged into a light raincoat and went for a walk. Big Ben chimed eight as he started out. He'd had no dinner. Angry again, Jackie refused to bother with it. Now he felt the pangs of hunger. He found a pub, ordered a lamb dinner, and sat back to relax. When the meal came, he thoroughly enjoyed the mint sauce served with the lamb, baked potatoes and cabbage greens. He'd almost finished when Jackie breezed in, sat at the bar and ordered a drink. If she'd seen him, she gave no indication.

Preston heard her joke with the bartender as if she'd been in many times. When he finished eating, he wondered what to do. Should he go over and speak to her? If he did, it would end the possibility of a nice, quiet walk. Contemplating took only a moment. As the cashier sat near the entrance, and Jackie had her back to the door, he chose the silent escape.

He strolled down the strand, then turned toward Buckingham Palace. Big Ben now struck nine-thirty, and with the heavy cloud cover, it was dark. The trees along the Mall stirred gently in the light breeze: a joyous song for the closing of day. Preston wished his heart could be so light. But he gave silent thanks for not having been able to marry Jackie, when he first felt the flush of desire. He'd be trapped now, and at the moment a hangman's noose seemed preferable.

He wondered how something that started out so wondrous could end so dismally. He felt certain Jackie had come to the same conclusion, but she would never admit to it.

Half-way down the Mall, he stopped to look up at the lights of a plane going north, probably to Birmingham or maybe Scotland. For a moment he wished he were a passenger on it, headed away from London. He'd always thought of London as a romantic city. Never again. Not with Jackie along.

Slowly, he began walking. Several young couples passed him, laughing as they hurried along. He envied them, but remembered his own age. The middle years, he told himself, with a messed up life and loneliness staring me in the face.

Pauline came to mind, living alone and miserable. She couldn't have Cole, so she wouldn't consider anyone else. Preston had always tried to help his sister, advising her about her finances and against her continuing passion to marry Cole, his business partner. But no amount of reasoning or caution seeped into her stubborn brain. She ignored it all, making a fool of herself, and a pest. Then her passion for frivolous things, cheap jewelry, worthless art and fur coats amazed him.

What Pauline wanted with two fur coats, he couldn't begin to guess, not with the rains that washed over Puget Sound and Seattle each year. "It's idiotic to own one here," he'd argued, "Let alone two."

"I need them," she'd told him.

"What for?"

After muttering to herself for a while, she'd replied, "How do you expect me to find a husband without them?"

How could he reason with such nonsense? He'd blinked and said no more, but he did wonder if the twist in her mind resembled the twist that had plagued an uncle years before. He barely remembered it, but he did remember his uncle not making any sense. He often answered a question with an unrelated statement. Pauline had been like that for some years, but was never cured.

As Preston approached the fence around the Palace, he paused. His hair, now soaked, released a rivulet of water that soaked his collar. He knew he should go back to the hotel, but the thought made his stomach knot. Instead, he turned toward St. James Park, then walked back along the Mall on the other side of the street.

Exhausted, he paused when he reached Trafalgar Square to look at the statue of Lord Nelson. It was gray with pigeon droppings. He wondered how often it had to be cleaned. Now completely soaked, he walked on to his office building. The office was dark, and after turning on one light, he took off his coat and sank down onto his chair. Big Ben chimed midnight. He leaned his head against the back of the overstuffed chair and promptly drifted off to sleep.

"But we really haven't given ourselves a chance," Jackie complained. Preston had come back in the wee hours of the morning. She'd not been able to sleep, fearing he'd already left her.

She'd done her best to avoid the present conversation, but she knew it had been coming for some time. Preston seemed determined to return to Seattle, saying the whole affair had been a miserable mistake. Though she had often thought he had regrets, she'd been determined to carry through with her plans to become Mrs. Leigh. She'd just come out of the shower, and stood in the doorway wrapped in a towel. "We need to give ourselves more time," she said, renewing the argument.

"More time won't help," he countered. "It was a mistake from the very start."

Indignant, she replied, "You never thought so when we first made love. You reveled in it, could hardly wait to get me alone." She intentionally spoke with harshness, determined to lay a guilt trip on him.

He wore a gray tweed suit with a blue striped tie as he prepared to leave for the office. His briefcase sat on the floor beside him. "As I remember it, you instigated the whole disgusting affair. I know I'm also to blame, but I never should have fallen for it."

"Who are you kidding? You were dying to have me long before I made it happen."

He blinked as if not understanding. "What? Where in the world did you get that preposterous notion?"

She slowly raised the towel and wiped away water running down her neck from her wet hair. He didn't take his eyes off her face as she tried to entice him.

"Where?" he demanded, sounding impatient.

"You ought to know. You confided in Pauline all the time." As she spoke, someone knocked at the door. "That's just my breakfast," she said, nodding for him to answer the door.

Amanda had arrived in London the afternoon before, and couldn't wait to get the horrid meeting with Preston over. She'd walked to the Savoy this morning, hoping to catch him before he went to work. Then she could leave this afternoon. She had no desire to see London. She knocked at the door and waited, a knot forming in her stomach.

"Amanda!" Preston gasped. He opened the door wide. Color immediately drained from his face.

"May I come in?" she asked in a stilted voice.

"Of course." He stepped aside.

She immediately spotted a startled, naked, Jackie at the bathroom door. So shocked at Amanda's presence, her mouth gaped, and her eyes seemed ready to pop out of her head.

"What the hell are you doing here?" Jackie shouted.

Furious, Amanda stared back. "Get out. I want to talk to Preston. Alone." Her stomach seemed to have risen to her throat, and anger sent blood racing through her. "How could you do this? How could you?" Amanda wanted to lash out at her, say words she'd never before allowed to slip from her tongue. But she wouldn't descend to that level. Instead, she fought for breath and the will to control her tongue. Jackie fled into the bathroom, slamming the door behind her. Amanda turned to Preston.

"Amanda," Preston said again, only now it came out in a whisper.

Standing before her was the man she'd adored, would have done anything for. But his recent actions ruled out any sense of pity or compassion for him. She felt anger, and the desire to hurt him, but couldn't find her voice.

"I wouldn't have had this happen for anything," he muttered.

After taking a deep breath, she replied, "Then why did you do it? You and this...what do I call her? I'd say a Tramp, a Nymphomaniac, a Slut? What would you call her?"

"Don't, Amanda. It's over. I swear it is." Beads of perspiration stood out on his face, and he looked ill enough to collapse.

"No, it's not. It never will be."

"But, Amanda, we could..."

"Don't even think it. Not after the way you betrayed me. You're no better than Jackie." Trembling, she paused to take another breath.

"I'm sorry." He plopped onto an overstuffed chair as if exhausted, while he studied her with wistful eyes.

Jackie threw open the bathroom door. In a pink satin bathrobe, she raced over to Preston, throwing her arms around his shoulders in a possessive hug. "What do you want?" she demanded of Amanda. "He's left you. Isn't that enough? Leave him alone. Stay out of our lives. Get out of our room." She released her grip on Preston.

With a forced laugh, Amanda said, "Unless I miss my guess, Preston paid for the room. You destroyed my life, and I won't leave until I tell you what a slut you are. A disgusting trollop." Jackie's mouth hardened as Amanda turned to Preston. "And you're a cheap excuse for a husband. You're a coward, a weakling." Venting her anger made it possible for her to think more clearly. Then to Jackie again, she said, "Milo will have a field day with this one, Jackie. Better get yourself a job. You'll need the money. No cushy life from now on."

With a broad smile, Jackie replied, "Preston will look after me. I don't need to worry."

"Not when I get through with him. He'll be looking for a second job to keep his head above water."

Preston lowered his head, his hands folded over the back of it, as if to fend off heavy blows.

"We'll make out," Jackie shot back. "Our love is forever." She lovingly stroked Preston's bent head.

He threw his hands in the air. "Don't, don't," he shouted as he jumped up and turned to face Jackie. "Don't touch me."

Jackie withered, pulling back, her face flushed.

Filled with the need to hurt them more, Amanda forced a smile. "Aren't you a delightful pair of adulterers?" She went to the door, opened it, then turned back to face Jackie. "Middle-aged love nests aren't what they're cracked up to be, are they? Too much baggage, one side or the another." She slammed the door behind her, took a deep breath to steady her nerves, then left the hotel.

Her own stepmother the other woman. The full impact of what had happened set in. She walked without knowing where, only that she had to put distance between herself and the two betrayers. Tears trickled down her cheeks as she kept wiping them away.

The morning was cool as she walked along, contrasting with the tears on her cheeks. Her head now ached, and her eyes felt sore, as if she'd been crying all night. She knew she'd been crying inside for weeks. No more, she told herself, but she couldn't lift the cloud from her mind. She found a bench in Hyde Park and sat a long time, trying to straighten out her thoughts. Never again did she want to speak to Preston or Jackie. Yes, Brooke had been right about getting an attorney to handle the mess. She wished she had done so.

CHAPTER 10

Desperate to show off her clothes and new hairstyle, Pauline dialed Amanda again, hoping to find her home. She seemed to be gone a long time. "Hello, Aunt Molly," she said, when someone answered the ring.

"I'm Hallie. My voice is much lighter and more pleasant than your Aunt Molly's." She chuckled.

"Sorry, Aunt Hallie. Has Amanda returned yet?"

"I expect she'll roll in sometime today. It wasn't a long vacation, but better than none. So, how are you doing, Pauline?"

"I'm just dying to show her my make-over. Tell her to call the moment she gets in. You're welcome to come over with her, see what I've accomplished." In her own mind, she'd completely changed her image.

"We've managed to do some shopping of our own," Hallie said, her voice ringing with pleasure.

Pauline thought Hallie might burst into song at any moment. She'd heard her sing many times, years before, in the farm store, and couldn't stand to hear it again. She responded with, "Overalls must be the same everywhere. Are they still gray? Or is it blue?" She felt a great deal of disgust, and didn't mind voicing it.

"Who said anything about overalls? I'm talking style here, the latest creations. That's what the saleswoman said. Why, we even shopped in one of those fancy lingerie boutique shops. Remarkable what they sell. The prices are much bigger than the items." She burst into a round of laughter. "Imagine me in a teddy." Again she laughed. "Haven't had so much fun since my courting days."

Pauline sighed, certain her Aunt's marbles were rattling. "They don't make teddies that big," she snapped.

"Why, we have most of our things custom made. Always a perfect fit. All we need now is someone to admire them. How about you?"

Cringing with disgust, Pauline ended the conversation with, "Sometime, perhaps. Be sure to tell Amanda to call me. Good-bye." She hung up. "Crazy old goat," she muttered through clenched teeth. Her mannequin friends nodded their agreement. "Why did they move here? To complicate my life? This has to be Preston's doings, with Amanda's help."

She stomped her way to the hall mirror to admire herself again. Her reflection mirrored the woman she wanted to be. "Meet the soon-to-be Mrs. Cole Martin," she bragged to the image, smiling broadly as she spoke. The image in the mirror seemed to shake her head. "But you're going to reject him."

"I'll marry him," Pauline shouted in defiance. "You just wait and see." But how could that be, if she intended to reject his proposal? Oh, well, she'd work that out later.

Preston had latched his suitcase, and looked at Jackie, who stood by the window, her back to him to hide her swollen eyes. "I've paid the rent for another week. You can suit yourself as to what you do."

After Amanda left yesterday, Preston finalized his plans. "I'm going back to Seattle to try and start over," he said.

Jackie burst into tears again. "Why don't you love me anymore?" she demanded, her lower lip in a pout.

The question would have caused Preston wrenching pains a few weeks ago. "I now know I never did. I'm sorry, but that's the way it is." He wished he didn't have to hurt her, but there seemed no other way.

"If Amanda hadn't butted into it..."

"No," he cut in. "That has nothing to do with my decision. I've tried to talk this out with you, but you always refused. Now, the decision is mine." He sat on the bed beside the suitcase.

She spun around to face him. "What am I supposed to do now? Crawl back to Milo?"

"Do whatever you want," he replied, "You always do."

"I can't, and it's all your fault." She began to weep loudly.

"How do you figure that?" He knew a tirade against Amanda was coming.

"If that bitch hadn't hunted you down, you'd still be happy with me."

Angered, Preston cautioned, "Watch who you're calling a bitch." He wanted to point out that she was the one who slept around, not Amanda. But he held his tongue.

"She frightened you, that's what." Then as if gaining strength from her accusations, she added, "You're a coward. That's what you are. A spineless coward."

He studied her for a moment. "You're right, Jackie. I left Amanda in a coward's way, but then so did you with Milo. I'll not act the coward again." Standing, he carried his suitcases to the door, returned for his wardrobe case and placed it on the chair near the door. He lifted the phone and called the front desk for assistance.

"You bastard," she flung at him. "You'll pay for this."

He shook his head. "I won't say it's been fun, Jackie." He removed an envelope from his jacket pocket and tossed it to her. "For your return trip."

A knock at the door drew his attention. He opened it and handed out the two cases, picked up the third and turned to Jackie. "Good luck."

"Go to hell," she shouted as he closed the door sharply behind him.

As the taxi pulled away, Amanda opened the front door of her home, dropped her suitcase inside the door, then closed it behind her with a sigh. The mid-afternoon sun hung low enough to put the house and yard in a welcome shade. As soon as she stepped on the tile entry, Molly called out, "Is that you, Amanda?"

Hallie hurried into the entry as Amanda answered, “Yes, and I’m bone tired.” Much to Amanda’s surprise, Hallie wore a gray denim skirt and yellow cotton shirt. She looked wonderful without the overalls.

“Goodness,” Hallie said. She gave Amanda a hug. “You do look tired.”

“Worn out,” Molly corrected. She’d come in from the kitchen wearing black slacks and a red plaid shirt. “I’ve about got supper ready. But you sit a while. Hallie, take her case up to her room for her.”

“Don’t worry about that,” Amanda said. “I can manage it later.” She moved her weary body to the sofa and plopped. She hadn’t slept on the flight home any more than on the flight out.

“But I can manage it now,” Hallie countered. “Just don’t tell Molly anything until I get back.” She grabbed the suitcase, tucked it under her arm and rushed up the stairs.

“How was the trip?” Molly asked, as she sat down beside Amanda.

Amanda thought she couldn’t explain without sounding bitter or bursting into tears. “Horrible,” she replied.

Hallie came bounding down the stairs and into the room. She stood watching for a second, then dropped to a chair opposite the others, and crossed her legs.

Immediately noticing the lace-up shoes, Amanda said, “No more boots? What you’re wearing looks far more comfortable. And your new clothes are great. You both look wonderful.”

Hallie proudly raised her foot, twisted it back and forth to give Amanda a good view, then said, “Looks much better, too, and easier to keep clean. I can get by nicely without boot-black.” Then catching her breath, she added, “You’ve got to see all the clothes we bought yesterday. Gave our old ones to Goodwill.”

“And good-riddance, too,” Molly said. “But that can wait. Did you see Preston?”

Amanda, her mood lightened, nodded. “And my infamous stepmother.”

Molly said, “I feared that.”

“Then you knew who Preston ran away with?” Too emotionally drained to show her anger, she closed her eyes.

"Oh, yes," Hallie said. "Watch out for that sister-in-law of yours, too. She's trouble no matter how you spell it. Always has been." Amanda opened her eyes to stare at Hallie.

"Now Hallie," Molly cut in. "We don't know that for a fact."

"Sure we do. That banshee told us things no woman should know about her brother and his wife."

"For heaven's sake, Hallie. Don't make things worse than they are."

Curiosity peeked, Amanda said, "Just what did Pauline tell you?"

"Nothing important. Just a pack of lies." Molly watched Amanda. "You do know she lies, don't you. A lot."

Amanda had often wondered about this. "Did she also tell you Preston was headed for London?"

Molly nodded, a look of resignation on her face.

"In London, he told me the affair was over, but Jackie still occupies his rooms. But it doesn't matter anymore. I can never trust him again."

"Were they registered as man and wife?" Hallie asked.

"What difference would that make?" Molly said, facing her sister. "Not the way they were living."

Hallie shrugged. "I guess not. By the way, Pauline called a couple of times. Wants you to call her. Claims she bought a stash of new clothes. Designer clothes, whatever that means. I thought all clothes were designed, more or less."

"She can worry about that later. Time for supper now," Molly cut in. She stood and headed for the kitchen.

Amanda stretched, then followed the two aunts, though she didn't feel hungry.

Jackie sat in her room at the Savoy, wondering what to do. Preston had left minutes before. She remembered with a shudder how Amanda had appeared unexpectedly. If Preston had gone on that trip to Paris, Amanda would have missed them, hence, no knowledge of his lover, and Jackie would be in the clear.

It's too late to worry about that now, she told herself. The fat's in the fire. She knew Milo would be furious, and the agreement she'd signed would preclude her from getting a large settlement in a divorce. So why seek a divorce? Then it dawned on her, Milo might well take her back, if he didn't know about her and Preston. Had Amanda blabbed about the affair? She had to know, so rushed to the phone. When Milo answered, she used her best exuberant voice to say, "Hello, darling."

"So, you finally called."

"Of course. I called to let you know I'm ready to come home." She took a deep breath and waited for his response.

"It's about time," he replied. "When will you get here?" He seemed a little angry, but she expected that.

With a sigh of relief, she replied, "I'm not sure yet. I'll catch the first flight I can. I hope it will be tomorrow. I'm so anxious to see you."

"I'm looking foreword to having you home."

"So am I. It's been too long, my darling."

"Whose fault is that?" he asked, rather stiffly.

She knew what she'd better say. "Mine, of course. But I won't ever stay away this long again."

"I'll say you won't. Next time you leave, I'm going with you."

When she hung up, Jackie rushed about to pack. She'd have to go to Paris and catch an overseas flight from there, just in case Milo ever checked.

Obviously Amanda hadn't told Milo what she found in London. She was a close-mouthed individual, never prone to discuss her affairs. And Preston? He wouldn't willingly admit to what he'd done. So she was probably safe. No repercussions, thank heavens. Life took on a new sheen.

CHAPTER 11

Amanda, Molly and Hallie drove into Seattle to visit Pauline. The whole time they wished to be doing something else, anything else.

"I'll be glad when this is over," Hallie grumbled. "I've never liked seeing Pauline, not since her visit to us when she was ten. Not that we wanted the visit. We'd already seen enough of her. Anyway, she was dumped on us for a whole month.

"I never knew that. I wonder why Preston never mentioned it," Amanda said.

"He probably doesn't remember it too well. He was seriously ill at the time. Pauline, though three years younger, tried to suffocate him with a pillow. If he hadn't been strong enough to shove her away, he'd be long dead."

Molly grunted, then added, "Wasn't the kind of child we wanted around, especially while we were working all day. Never knew just what she was up to."

"That's awful," Amanda gasped. "Why would she try to kill Preston?" Did the aunts actually know what they were talking about?

"Like I always said, she's got some bolts missing," Hallie volunteered from the back seat. "She never told why she did it. Even claimed Preston lied about it. If we'd doubted Preston before her visit, we certainly didn't afterward."

"Why?" Amanda asked. "What happened?"

Molly replied, "No need to go into it all, but she stole from the store, hiding the items in her room. Not that she needed anything, and the things she took were of no use to her. Tools and the like. And then she abused the cats we kept in the store, and deliberately left items on the stairs for us to trip over."

"Preston once said she needed special attention, when she was a child. I thought she was sickly."

"Tell her the rest," Hallie pressed. "She might just as well know it."

Amanda took a quick glance at Molly, who sat beside her.

"She gets the picture," Molly chided. "Let's not drive it into the ground."

"She needs to know," Hallie insisted. "Only one in the family whose clock is short an hour. Been short since her birth."

Again Amanda looked at Molly. They had just driven up to the curb in front of Pauline's house. "Tell me before we go inside." Thinking it couldn't be anything worse than what she'd just been told, she added, "Prepare me."

Molly pursed her lips, twisting them from side to side, as if pondering what to say. "She was suspected of being involved in the death of another child in Idaho. That's why the family moved to Washington."

"Involved how?" Amanda felt a cold chill at the back of her neck.

"We never learned that," Hallie replied. "And ever since, I won't be left alone with her, so you two stick to me like glue."

"Oh, Hallie," Molly chided. She opened the door and got out. Then turning to Amanda, said, "They institutionalized her for a while. Said she was cured."

As they walked up the front path, the house now seemed foreboding. Three wooden shutters hung lopsided by two windows, and the panes were small and dirty. To Amanda, the home had always looked sinister, something from the "Adam's Family" TV series. Yet, Preston's parents seemed to love the place.

To lighten the mood, Amanda joked, "I suppose the attic is full of wingless bats, the missing parts steeping in a pot over the kitchen stove?"

All were laughing when Pauline opened the front door.

"Come in, Amanda," Pauline said, stepping aside. She nodded to the twin aunts, her way of greeting them. "I've a lot to show you." She stroked her short hair as if to straighten it, but the hair was far too short to make any difference.

Amanda stared at the new hairstyle. On Pauline it looked grotesque, accentuating her sharp features. She mentally questioned the state of Pauline's sanity.

The drab hallway, which had recently been covered with brown and green flowered wallpaper, had a ceiling light, no brighter than a 40-watt bulb, which turned the brown into somber shadows.

Amanda hadn't been in the house for over a year. Whenever she and Preston went to see Pauline, she insisted they meet at a pizza parlor near her home. Neither Preston nor Amanda had understood why.

"Come up to my room," Pauline purred, as she led the way up the brown carpeted stairs. Molly and Hallie rolled their eyes and grimaced at the suggestion, though only Amanda saw it.

"In here." With an expectant smile, she opened the door and stepped inside.

Amanda's stared in disbelief. Six mannequins stood at attention along one wall, stiff and staring straight ahead. A brown striped slouch suit hung on one. A cream sleeveless dress with a jagged hem, clothed the second. A third wore a one-button blouse, not meant to hide anything, and a mini skirt of orange silk. All were attired in clothes inappropriate for Seattle life, as far as Amanda was concerned. And one wore a wedding gown of lace.

Each mannequin wore a different wig, black, blond, chestnut, auburn, brown and strawberry blond. One wig matched Pauline's hairstyle. Almost bald, the face beneath it looked cruelly haggard, and unnaturally made up with thick red paint on the lips, and blotchy pink rouge on the cheeks. It looked grotesque. Good heavens, she's really gone nuts, Amanda thought.

"Aren't these clothes wonderful?" Pauline purred. "I had to hunt all over New York to get exactly what I wanted. They're like pictures in the fashion magazines, don't you think?" She paused to catch her breath. "This one is Charlotte," she said, pointing to the first mannequin. "Then Twilla, Gretchen, Amelia, Claudette and Rosemary. She's the one that had the baby. Remember?" She pointed to each as she spoke the names. "Aren't they adorable?" She talked as if they were beloved friends, all-standing at attention to be introduced.

Hallie glanced at her twin with a look of alarm, and said, "But where the devil can you wear clothes like these?" Her mouth twisted in distaste.

Molly nudged her sister in the ribs. "They certainly are different," she said. "Is this the fashion in New York?"

"Of course. The fashion houses wouldn't make them, if they didn't sell." Then turning to Hallie, Pauline said, "I wouldn't expect anyone from Montana to recognize style."

Still, as if in shock, Hallie replied, "I have to see it first." Again Molly nudged her sister hard enough to make Hallie wince.

"She's just jealous," Molly explained. "Never mind her. She's too heavy for this delicate collection, anyway."

"Oh, I don't mind her. What do you think of it, Amanda?" Pauline's full attention turned to Amanda.

At a loss for words, she finally replied, "Well, they certainly make you look twice."

"You bet they do, and just wait until...everyone... sees me in them." Her face glowed as if she were about to burst into song.

"Everyone? Anyone in particular?" Knowing Pauline's crush on Cole, Amanda thought Pauline had him in mind.

Pauline smiled broadly. "This is part of my trousseau."

Shocked, Amanda stared at Molly and Hallie, while Hallie gasped, "You don't say."

Amanda spoke up. "Are you serious?"

"Of course. Why wouldn't I be?" She walked to a hanger in the closet and began stroking the lace of a chiffon negligee hanging there. "I'm sure...he'll love me in this creation. Won't be able to take his eyes off me."

Molly and Hallie took a furtive glance at each other.

"They're all lovely, Pauline," Hallie said. "Just lovely."

With an unbelieving stare, Pauline eyed Hallie up and down. "That's not what you said a while ago. What changed your mind?"

Hallie, pale and looking nervous, stammered, "A...a second look. A closer second look." She caught Amanda's eye and nodded toward the door.

Though she felt uneasy, Amanda tried not to show it. "I can see you made careful choices, Pauline." Never before had she feared Preston's sister, but now Amanda shivered. What the aunts had said on the way over didn't help. Pauline needed medical attention. She'd never dated for years, so where was this man she intended to marry? The only man that came to mind was Cole Martin, and he couldn't stand Preston's sister.

With distrustful eyes, Pauline said, "I expected you to call me last night, Amanda."

"She was tired," Molly quickly explained. "We fed her and sent her to bed."

"Where did you go?" Her darkened eyes had a glassy look about them, and they seemed unnaturally large.

"Canada." Again Molly cut in before Amanda could speak.

Amanda went along with it, nodding.

"You'll have to tell us all about it when we get home, Amanda," Molly said. "We've never been to Canada."

"I'll do just that." Amanda thought the questioning would end with her statement, but Pauline wasn't finished.

"Has Preston called you?" She stood stroking the lace on her fancy gown. "This is my wedding gown," she said, her fingers fondly moving over the lace.

Hallie ambled toward the door, then said, "When is the wedding?"

Spinning around to glare at Hallie, she replied, "That's a secret. It's all a secret."

"We won't tell anyone," Amanda promised, now very concerned for Pauline. She'd seen Pauline in odd moods before, but this one topped all the others.

"I asked if you'd heard from Preston?" Pauline demanded, her tone offensive.

"No," Amanda replied, "He hasn't called me. I don't expect he will."

Pauline's expression softened. "Good. He mustn't know about my wedding. He'll just try to stop it. Nothing I do pleases him. He really hates me, but keeps it hidden from the rest of you. But if he interferes, I know how to handle him."

"I doubt he hates you, Pauline," Molly volunteered.

"What the hell do you know?" Pauline shot back, her face again tight, and her eyes beady black. "You've never been under his thumb, never lived with him."

"At any rate, I've left a stew on the stove. We'll have to leave or it will be scorched beyond eating."

The swift mood change in Pauline set Amanda's mind racing. What caused it? Why did it happen?

Pauline led the way down the stairs and to the front door. Molly and Hallie quickly stepped out, but Pauline grabbed Amanda's arm, detaining her for a moment.

"Is it really awful?" she whispered.

"What do you mean?" Amanda couldn't guess at what was going through Pauline's mind.

"That first night with someone else taking up half of the bed?" She looked worried, her forehead in ridges, and her voice thin and raspy.

"No," Amanda replied, feeling sorry for Pauline. "It isn't awful at all."

Preston sat in Cole's office, feeling like an idiot, but determined to eat humble pie. "I remember you telling me how foolish I was. I wish I'd listened. Anyway, I couldn't stand being with Jackie any longer." Cole watched with squinting eyes. "I've no idea why I didn't see what could happen. Heaven knows I'd seen enough of her to realize her antics wouldn't change."

Cole leaned back on his chair, crossed his legs and cupped his chin in one hand. "And now what? What about Amanda?"

Preston sighed, then related what had happened in London. "I've destroyed any love she had for me, and I don't blame her. I'll get an apartment here in town, then perhaps take over one of the buyer's jobs. I'd be out of town most of the time, only needing a small place."

"What about your house?"

"It's Amanda's. I'll see she's well taken care of."

"You're running away, aren't you?" He brushed his thick, curly hair from his forehead.

The door opened and Amanda took a step in before she froze at the sight of Preston.

"Come in, Amanda," Cole said. Both men stood as she walked to a chair facing Cole.

Amanda looked stunning in a blue dress and matching jacket. Her blonde hair hung loosely at shoulder length. Preston had to catch his breath, the old desire mounting in him.

"What can I do for you, Amanda?" Cole asked, as soon as Amanda was seated.

Without looking at Preston, she replied, "I'm not sure. And I might have made a mistake in coming here."

"You'll never do that, Amanda," Cole said. Like Amanda, he seemed to be ignoring Preston.

"I wanted you to contact Preston."

Cole said, "But he's here. You can tell him yourself." He glanced at Preston and nodded.

"Well," she began, "I suppose it's just as well." She slowly faced her husband, as if reluctant to look at him.

"What is it?" Preston asked, hoping to make it easier for her.

"It's Pauline."

"What about her?"

Amanda adjusted herself on the chair before she spoke again. "She needs medical help."

Preston found it odd that Amanda would make such a statement. "She has a doctor," he replied. "A very good one."

Amanda rubbed her thin, delicate fingers over her arms. "She tells me she's getting married."

"That's ridiculous," Preston replied. The statement wouldn't seem so strange, if Pauline ever dated. She never had, though she'd often told him she wanted to marry Cole. "She was teasing you," he added.

"Then why did she go to New York to buy a trousseau?"

He saw the worried look on Amanda's face, and it disturbed him. "When did you hear this?" He straightened, leaning closer to her.

"She told me two days ago."

"She had to be teasing," Preston replied.

"She told me in front of Molly and Hallie."

"My God! Are they here?"

Cole looked from one to the other, obviously interested in the conversation, and looking worried.

"They're here at your invitation. Didn't you invite them to move out this way when they sold the feed store?"

"Are they staying with Pauline?" He certainly hoped so.

"You know better than to think that. They're with me." Her voice quivered as she spoke.

Preston didn't know if her anger caused it, or the presence of his aunts. "How long have they been here?"

"Some time...a few weeks." She averted her eyes now, turning to face Cole.

"I'm sorry they landed on you. I should have been here," Preston apologized.

"Yes." She didn't look at him.

"I'll take care of my aunts as soon as I can."

"You don't need to do anything. They're fine with me, and Pauline wouldn't begin to treat them kindly."

He nodded. "Did you think Pauline was serious about getting married? Not just imagining?"

Now she glared at him. "Preston! Imagining or not, she needs help, and the way she acted was most peculiar. Then there is her selection of clothes. All inappropriate. You know she's always been crazy about Cole. Now she thinks she's going to marry someone, who else?"

"That's ridiculous," he muttered, though he began to worry in earnest.

"Then who? That trousseau is real. And the negligee."

Cole cleared his throat loudly several times. "Just a moment, here. What makes you think she's talking about me? I've never liked her, only dated her once years ago. I never see her, thank God." He moved to the edge of his chair, shock distorting his face. "Frankly, I can't stand the sight of her." He spoke slowly, as if to emphasize his feelings. He nervously released the knot in his tie.

"You've got to be mistaken, Amanda." Preston began to sweat, his shirt collar feeling too tight, his jacket sleeves binding against his shirt. He prayed the whole business was somehow a mistake. Could it be happening again?

"No," she replied, shaking her head. "Your aunts told me a few things you neglected to tell me about her past. Why didn't you ever tell me she'd been in an institution?"

He felt cornered. He'd never told her for fear she'd dislike his sister. Pauline had been fine for some years now, he thought. Or had she? "I'll check on it soon," he said, though his inner senses told him he'd have to do something, perhaps have her committed again. He'd consult her doctor first.

"You aren't listening, Preston. Pauline needs help. Now! She should have had it sooner, but you were too busy with your...." She let the words fade away, but not the anger. "Do something before she gets into real trouble."

Preston's stomach churned until he ached all over. His head began to pound, his eyes smart. What was he to do? His aunts needed attention, his sister needed help, and his wife...his wife hated him. He could see it on her face, in her eyes. Then in the background sat Milo, who probably would kill Preston, if he knew what had happened. "Did you tell Milo about Jackie and me?"

"That's up to you to work out," she replied. "Jackie and you can tell him all the lies you like. I'll not interfere, but forget them for the time being. Take care of Pauline first."

Cole leaned back against the chair, still looking worried.

Preston didn't want to think of Pauline, only Amanda. How else could he straighten out his life, his future? "We need to talk."

"About what?" she demanded.

Cole watched her closely, his eyes squinting.

"Us," Preston replied.

"There is no us," she said. "Only me. Out there somewhere in the mist is you, a you I no longer know, and don't want to know. And if you don't take the time to see Pauline gets medical help, you'll find it's too late, just like it is with me." She stood to leave. Cole saw her to the door, while Preston stood rigid beside the desk.

"Take care," Cole said as he touched her arm. She smiled and left.

Preston, now deeply concerned for his sister, determined to visit her first, check on her, and then consult her doctor. What a damned mess my life is in, he thought.

CHAPTER 12

When Preston arrived to see his aunts, Amanda quietly left by the back door. She'd been stunned to see him in Cole's office yesterday, and for a few moments she'd felt her heart stop beating.

She'd thought about it all night, and concluded time would soften the hurt. She'd also decided to move out of the house, allowing Preston to return. He and his aunts could live together, for a while. In the meantime, she could rent an apartment at Preston's expense. When she'd earned her degree, she'd move to Portland to be near Brooke. She didn't want to be near Preston, and her solution would help everyone concerned.

The remaining problem was Pauline. What would Preston do about her? Institutionalization seemed the only option, but then Preston had the say in that. Though she wasn't sure he believed her yesterday, when he got around to visiting Pauline he'd understand Amanda's concern.

Now she began to wonder about Jackie. And what about Milo, and the harp? Would Jackie wait in Europe for it, or had she returned with Preston? At the moment, she'd like to think the harp had been lost in transit. Since returning from London, she'd thrown away all the tapes of Jackie playing the harp, feeling too much anger and bitterness to listen to any of them again.

She drove to her father's house, desirous to know if Jackie had returned. As no divorce had been filed, for Milo had not called her to complain, she felt Preston wouldn't live openly with Jackie in Seattle. So if she'd returned, where had she temporarily hung her hat?

Agatha opened the door for Amanda. "Well," she beamed. "It's nice to see you again. You don't visit half enough."

She gave Agatha a hug. "You know how my visits go with Dad." She shrugged. "How's his mood today? Is he aching for a fight?"

With a grimace, Agatha whispered. "Not too bad a mood, but 'Her Highnose'" is coming home in a few days. That keeps him happy, for a while."

Amanda laughed. Agatha had called Jackie, "Her Highnose" ever since Jackie moved into the house, behind Jackie's back, of course.

"Milo's on the patio at the library door." She nodded the direction. Her usual brown dress and white apron, a uniform Jackie insisted she wear to keep her in her place, were gone today. Instead, she wore a blue dress.

"You look terrific in blue," Amanda said, as she paused before going outside. "But what will Jackie say when she gets home?"

Agatha laughed. "I don't care...if she doesn't like it, she can find another... another...whatever I am around here. A cook? A housekeeper? A maid? No, just a lackey for Jackie. But you know, with just your father here, life is certainly less complicated, and I enjoy it. With 'Her Highnose' about," she paused to make a face, "Well, I'm not sure I'm going to take much more. Guess I'm the one aching for a fight."

"What in the world for?" Amanda asked, concerned that Agatha might actually quit.

"Is that you, Amanda?" Milo's demanding voice came from the patio. "Hurry up and come out here."

Anger pent up from her youth swelled as she listened to his orders. Anger she'd never dared vent, and now she swallowed it again. "I'll be right there," she called out. "A fight with whom?" she softly asked Agatha.

"That...that scarlet woman who married your father for security and spending money." She looked drained as she spoke. "But he don't know the difference. That's what hurts the most. He's blind in one eye, and can't see out of the other," she complained.

"Amanda?" Milo called again.

She winced, but managed to squeeze Agatha's hand in sympathy. "We'll talk later." She wondered how much Agatha knew about Jackie?

Before going outside, she paused to take a deep breath, than as Amanda walked outside, Milo said, "Why don't you come to see me more often? I'm your father." He turned from the paper as Amanda sat down on the chair beside him.

"I've been terribly busy," she explained, upset further by her father's tone of voice. "Preston's two aunts are visiting. Looking for a place to live." She hoped to keep the conversation on an even keel for both their sakes.

"Therefore too busy to see me?" A superficial pout curled his mouth.

"Dad," she began to explain, "You had little time for me before. We've never been close." Her resolve began to crumble as his anger mounted.

"But that was years ago," he argued. "I was awfully busy then, but I gave you a new mother." A look of satisfaction spread across his face, though his eyes remained dark.

"What mother?" she demanded. "Jackie was only your new plaything, not my mother. And the both of you let me know I was in the way." She paused to take a breath and calm her emotions. This was a score never settled between them, and she didn't want to go into it now. "So, how are you?"

He seemed to have ignored her statement. "Waiting for my angel to come home. She's taking her good and ready time about it, if you ask me." He tossed the newspaper aside, and watched it flutter to the patio stones. He sat in a brown smoking jacket, striped brown trousers and felt slippers.

"Then you've heard from Jackie lately." Amanda set her purse beside the chair as she talked.

"Yesterday. She's coming home as soon as she can get a flight." His tone became petulant. "Then I'll find out what took her so long." He stared out across the lawn as he spoke, his eyebrows knit.

The expansive lawn had just been mowed, and the grassy odor lingered. Amanda had always loved the refreshing smell. As a child, she'd followed the hired man on his mower as he went round and round, cutting and trimming. The rhododendrons lining the lawn were much larger now, stretching out over part of the lawn.

The kidney-shaped swimming pool, in the center of the lawn, had been drained and looked like a huge, gaping mouth waiting for something to eat. "Why the dry pool?" she asked.

"Hell, there's no one to use it. No need to keep wasting chlorine."

"Dad," she began, angry again at his tone of voice, and his love of money. "You need to exercise. You use it, instead of sitting around all day, griping and getting fatter."

His head swung around to face her. "What's this? You came over here to criticize me? Boss me about?"

"Boss you about? What a laugh! When could anyone do that? But to get back to the point, you're always grousing about Jackie's lovers. Well, get up and do something to make yourself more presentable to her." She started to say more, but forced herself to stop, though it proved difficult.

"And just what do you suggest?" he demanded, his voice loud enough for Agatha to hear, no matter where she might be. As he talked, a cat walked across the lawn and lay down not far from the chairs. "Damned cat," he blurted out. Removing one of his slippers, he threw it hard, but the cat jumped and scurried away.

Amanda didn't recognize the cat. "Whose is it?"

Short of breath from his brief exertion, he replied, "Agatha's. Always gets in the way."

She scoffed. "It does not, but if you think so, get up off the chair and chase it, but one way or another, don't sit so much." She now let her anger get the best of her. "And more to the point, you're three times the size you ought to be. A perfect candidate for a heart attack, that's you, always moping about over Jackie. She's not worth it."

"Hell, girl. Don't try to tell me what to do."

Angered beyond any sense of restraint, she countered, "Someone has to tell you, or you won't make old bones." Filled with disgust at herself for what she's said, as well as for her father goading her into it, she stood and walked away.

He called to her. "Amanda, sit down for a moment. We need to talk." His whole demeanor had changed so quickly it startled her. She couldn't remember the last time he'd been so polite to her.

"Something's wrong. You never talked to me like that before. You've always been so quiet and understanding. What is it?"

She sat down again, but for a moment she didn't know how to respond.

"Is Preston back?" he asked.

"Yes, he's back."

Milo frowned. "Are the two of you having trouble?"

Her father had never given any concern to her affairs, not as a child, not as a teen, not as an adult. Why suddenly now? She didn't welcome his nosy concern. "Since when did you care?" She eyed him critically, his massive body, his three chins, his fat hands.

"Don't get snippy again," he snapped, his face turning red.

Steeling herself, she replied, "Everything is fine with me."

"Too much work with the company, I suppose."

Rather than say anything to give away the problem, she replied, "Probably."

"Get some help, Amanda. Preston can afford to do that much for you."

His face showed concern she'd never before seen. It puzzled her. Her thoughts went to the prospect of a smaller place. She'd like to be near Brooke soon, not in a year or two. The children Brooke was going to adopt would help keep her mind off the problems confronting her. Perhaps she'd wait a year before returning to school, take a good long time to unwind, to escape this worrisome environment. "I'll soon have my problems solved," she replied. "One way or the other."

Pauline spent a great deal of time looking at her new wardrobe, and scheming to land Cole. She'd wanted to ask Amanda to go to his office with her, but she couldn't, not with the old aunts present. But she could certainly do it over the phone. Admiring her clothes again, she put on the negligee and danced about for a few minutes, then went to a mirror and admired herself. "You're beautiful," Rosemary said, "Any man should want you."

Pauline laughed with satisfaction. Finally, she went down to the phone, still wearing the negligee. When Preston answered, her breath caught in her throat, and she could barely breathe. Why was he back?

"Who is this?" he asked, when she didn't respond to his hello.

"What are you doing there? You're supposed to be in London. Why aren't you?" How could he do this to me?

"I've moved back," he replied. "What did you call for, Pauline. Do you have a problem?"

His voice seemed cold, uncaring, and she dreaded the implications. Had he found out what she'd done? "I just want to talk to Amanda," she finally said, though her throat had become tight and dry.

"She's not here. Gone out for a while. How are you, Pauline?"

"Just fine," she muttered, not knowing exactly what to say. "Yes, I'm just fine. Are you back with Amanda?"

He didn't respond for several seconds. "Looks that way, doesn't it?"

She felt panic stricken, breaking into a heavy sweat. Had Jackie told him, after promising not to? Did he know what the two had cooked up? She remembered his reaction years ago, when she advised him not to marry Amanda. God! She didn't want to go through that again. She'd lied and connived to prevent the marriage, then Preston had found out. They'd fought for hours, him trying to get her to apologize to Amanda. She refused, and Preston proved too much of a gentleman to tell Amanda about it. Even as she tried to mull over the words, they became confused. She wasn't sure her accusations weren't true. Her mind often became hazy on such matters.

Years before, when her parents told her she'd tried to smother Preston, while he was ill in bed, she never believed them. Over the years, she thought everyone lied to her. And from the moment she could talk, she resented her brother. That much she'd remembered clearly, or thought she did.

"Are you still there?" Preston asked.

"Of course."

"Good. I want to talk to you. I'll be over in about an hour. And I mean to your place, not some restaurant."

"Of course," she replied. "I'll have a drink ready for you." He'd sounded angry, and she wished she had something to put in his drink.

"No drink," he said rather sharply. "Only talk."

So many things she had to do before he arrived. "See you," she said, then hung up. She rushed up to her bedroom. One by one she removed the mannequins, trudging up the rickety pull-down stairs to her hiding room, and explaining her actions to each one as she went. "He won't notice anything," she promised. "He'll never understand why you're here, that you're my friends. I won't let him send you away." She'd caught the negligee on the corner of the top railing. When she discovered a tear, she began to cry. She changed it for a sweater and slacks, then hung the negligee on a mannequin, still sorrowing over the rip.

Teary eyed, she waited in the living room. As she waited, her mind became confused, her thoughts disoriented. Who was coming to see her? She couldn't remember, but she knew she had to be very careful of what she said to the visitor. The visitor she hated, but couldn't avoid.

CHAPTER 13

Milo stomped about the patio, cursing under his breath, the patio stones trembling beneath his feet. He'd just received a call from an investigator that he'd hired to trace Jackie. After weeks of waiting, he'd finally called. The information infuriated him, and he began sweating as his heels clicked on the stones. "What the hell does she take me for?" he muttered. Back and forth he went, mind racing. Too bad Jackie hadn't produced any children, then she'd have had to stay home, or would she? She didn't want to raise Amanda. Agatha had done that, good old Agatha. She's worth her weight in gold.

He plopped onto a chair. What about that damned harp? Had he sent it soon enough for her to receive it? She cared more for it than for him. And what about Amanda? Had she taken back Preston? He sure as hell wouldn't take Jackie back. Not this time. All desire for her had been killed.

But he knew she'd return contrite, head bowed, words of regret flowing readily from her lips, as always. It was different now, since she'd also betrayed his daughter as well. How could she do such a thing? What a damned fool Preston had been.

Now he understood Amanda's dislike of Jackie. Yes, trusty old Agatha had raised his daughter, and he felt very kindly toward her. Wouldn't fire her when Jackie demanded he do so. No sir!

Again he paced, and the patio became far too small. He headed out across the lawn, kicking at the few fallen leaves from the old oak at the far corner of the yard. On his return trip, he paused to look at the empty pool. By damn, he'd have it filled tomorrow and begin swimming again. Not for Jackie's sake, but for his own. It had been a couple of years since he'd felt good physically. He hadn't told anyone, but he suspected his heart might soon cause problems, if he didn't change his ways.

He'd swim all right, and start walking as well. To hell with Jackie! He'd given up caring any more. However, it did infuriate him to know she'd returned to her old tricks, even after signing that document promising not to do so. He should have known better than to trust anything she said. Now the marriage was over.

With Jackie returning soon, he had to give a great deal of thought as to what he'd do. When he reached the patio, he plopped onto the chair again, puffing as if he'd run a mile. His chest heaved and hurt a little, and he wondered if he'd already left things too long. But soon his breathing returned to normal, and he forgot about it.

Jackie could return as early as tomorrow, and he felt repulsion. Why couldn't she have had some of Agatha's qualities? Trustworthy. Reliable. Good old Agatha. A good cook, too.

He brought his mind back to the problem at hand. He realized Jackie hadn't had time to collect her harp. He'd sent it freight. Good. She could go without her damned harp. He found himself smiling broadly, then laughing out loud. "Serves her right," he chuckled. Then he decided to call the hotel and tell them to give it to some musical society.

Agatha had silently come onto the patio. "What's tickling your fancy?" she asked.

Still smiling, he said, "I think I've finally gotten rid of that harp. Lost in transit." He laughed again.

"Good for you," she said. "Can I do anything for you?"

"Yes. Sit down and help me decide what to do. How do I get Jackie out of here?" Agatha looked puzzled, so he added, "When she comes home."

"Sure you want to?" She sat on the other chair beside the table, waiting expectantly.

"Hell, yes."

A subtle smile betrayed her pleasure as she watched him, one eyebrow raised. "No regrets later?"

"Regrets? You can't imagine how many I already have, starting with Amanda. There isn't room for any more. No regrets concerning Jackie."

"Good. Then you leave it to me. I know exactly how to handle her." With a her jaw set firmly she added, "Yes, sir! It will be a pleasure." She looked directly into his eyes. "Sure you want it done?"

Squinting and wandering what tack she would use, he nodded firmly. "You bet."

When Preston arrived to talk to Pauline, her face showed strain, and the lines around her mouth were tight, as if she were angry with him. She wore a clinging, short black leather skirt, and a low-cut blue silk blouse. "What in heaven's name did you do to yourself? And these walls?" he demanded, looking around. "The whole damned place looks more like a dungeon than a house. And you...I can't believe it." He stood just inside the door, his eyes scanning the place.

"I like it, and myself," she defended, her mind now clear. "And it's my house. I can do what I please with it." She turned her back to him and marched on high heel into the living room. Then turning to face him, she demanded, "So why are you here? Why the need for a talk?"

Again Preston eyed the drab room with distaste. It looked as if it had been prepared for a funeral. "Good grief, Pauline. There are other colors besides brown."

"If you don't like it, you can leave," she shouted. "I never asked you to come."

Now he studied her face more closely. Rigid with anger, it was far from normal. Her sharp-boned features were uniquely pale, her eyes ringed with dark shadows and hollow. And her hair? "Pauline," he began, "Are you all right?"

"Of course!" she shot back. "I've never been better." She pursed her lips to show the extent of her contempt for him.

"Sit down, Pauline," he said in a kindly voice. They both sat on the green sofa, facing each other. "Amanda said you'd been to New York to buy clothes."

"I went there," she stiffly replied.

"And your hair? Did you have it shaved there?" The moment the words were out, he regretted them.

"It isn't shaved. This is the new fall fashion." She patted her head with both hands, emphasizing her contentment with the style.

He'd been so taken back with the changes she'd made to their childhood home, he felt anger, though he had no right to. Controlling it wasn't easy. "Where are the clothes you bought in New York?" He wanted to see them for himself before making a judgment. "And the mannequins. May I see them?"

"Amanda told you I bought clothes? She doesn't listen very well, does she? I told her I'd travel to Paris in the fall for new clothes. I couldn't find what I wanted in New York. What a laugh she is. Never gets things straight."

Preston felt confused. She had bought clothes because even the Aunts had told him so. They, too, had seen them. And how about this supposed marriage? "Are you seeing anyone? Have you been dating?" He hoped she didn't show any signs of illness, as Amanda had indicated. He didn't want to go through what his parents had many years ago. They had her confined for over a year, but she didn't improve. She blamed Preston for the confinement, accused him of lying to their parents about her.

In her early twenties, Pauline had quit her job as a sales clerk, and stayed at home, hiding whenever anyone came to the house. For over a year she played the hermit, before her hospitalization again. Then slowly she began to come back to reality.

Preston realized she hadn't answered his question. "No boyfriend?" he ventured again.

"Of course I have boyfriends. I'm not some sort of freak, you know. I'm as normal as you."

"I never said you weren't normal." But he wasn't so sure. Deep in her eyes, he could see hints of the old confusion. "Have you seen our aunts?" He knew she had, but had to keep the conversation going. Get her to talk. Perhaps then make a decision.

"Yes, I've seen them. They're still very homely, and dress like men. A total disgrace to the family." She spoke with curled lips. "Will Amanda take you back? I wouldn't do it if it were me."

Unexpected anger rose within him. "That's not any of your business." Jackie's words came to mind again. She'd said, "You always confided in Pauline." He never had, nor would. But now he felt sure Pauline had been stirring up trouble again.

"It's none of your business about my affairs," she snapped. "Remember that."

"I only want to help you," he said.

"Oh, sure. Like when you told our parents I wanted to kill you." She stood and walked to the door. "I have things to do, so if you'll excuse me..." The words trailed off, but she faced him again. "If I need your help, I'll let you know. I already have six excellent advisers."

"What?" Who in the world is she talking about?

"You heard me. The very best one is Rosemary."

"Rosemary? Rosemary who?" Astonished, Preston didn't understand why he'd never heard of her.

"You don't need to know."

"But I want to," he replied. "I need to understand." He found himself perspiring heavily.

"That's not why you came here." She stood in the doorway, waiting for him to leave. When he didn't stand, she added, "You can't stop me from marrying, you know. You aren't my guardian."

He shook his head. "You never told me you were thinking of marriage." Now his worries grew deeper. "With whom?"

"When I want you to know, I'll tell you. Now go!"

Preston went out the front door without looking back. He sat in the car for a long time, trying to understand his sister, make sense of her actions. Before he drove out off, he looked up at the second floor window of Pauline's bedroom. The curtains were pulled back and two faces peered out at him. Pauline and…a mannequin?

"I get the girls," Brooke was saying to Amanda. Excitement caused her to talk loudly.

Amanda had called to ask about it. "When? How soon?"

"Next week. I can hardly wait. Mrs. Beck has already moved in here. We're all set up and ready to go get them. Mrs. Beck...I mean Nadine is wonderful. I'm lucky to get her."

"Sounds like it. When can I meet your new family?" Amanda felt anxious, too, but very happy for her friend.

"How about two weeks. That should give us time to get to know each other. Blend into the house."

"Hey," Amanda said. "I'm jealous." She did feel a few pangs, wishing she and Preston had had children.

After a moment, Brooke said, "So what are you going to do about school?"

"I'm not sure right now. I don't want to stay around here. I'm thinking of moving to Portland."

"We've lots of choices here, as far as colleges are concerned," Brooke replied. "You could easily get what courses you need, or you could even change your major. Will you need to work and go to school at night?"

"No. Preston can pay the rent for an apartment, and support me until I get a degree."

"Then you'd better get started on that divorce. I'd love to have you living closer. What a lot of fun we could have."

"I'll see an attorney tomorrow." Then Amanda went on to explain what had happened in London, and of Preston's return to Seattle. "My own stepmother! Can you believe it?"

Brooke laughed, then apologized. "Sorry about the laughter. I know it really isn't funny, but Preston must have been wearing horse blinders. Jackie's face tells all there is to know about her. She's one warped cookie. Does your father know? Is she still his 'angel'?"

"Yes, he believes she is."

"Even after what's happened? I can't believe it."

"He doesn't know what's happened. I haven't the heart to tell him." She'd thought to tell him many times, but couldn't bring herself to do so.

"Has Jackie come back to him?"

"Seems as though she's going to."

"What nerve! How will you ever face her again?"

"That's one more reason to leave here. I get angry every time I think about what the two have done." Seeing Jackie would never let her anger die. As for Preston, even his name triggered another form of anger, like the anger she harbored toward her father, who continually pushed her into the background to make points with Jackie. She couldn't swallow it down. Total betrayal. She felt as betrayed now as then.

CHAPTER 14

Jackie took a cab from the airport, anxiety keeping her tense and perspiring. Has Amanda told Milo about London? she wondered. The closer the cab got to Seattle, the more worries came to mind. What if Milo sued for a divorce? If he did, would she get much money out of it? Not if Milo had his way. Would he want a messy divorce? She knew she didn't, but would make it so, if Milo pressed her too hard.

Heavy rain started to fall, and traffic moved more slowly than she'd hoped. More time to worry over Milo's reception. Perhaps she had nothing to worry about. She brightened. After all, he'd forgiven her the other times. Why not this one, if he knew about it? Convincing herself of his unconditional love, she thought he'd eagerly welcome his angel home. But slivers of doubts kept pricking her conscience.

A stern-faced Agatha opened the door for her. Jackie said, "Hello," softly, as if not to disturb some sleeping giant. "Where's Milo?" she asked, dropping her purse to a chair. Without waiting for an answer, she said, "There are several cases to be brought in, Agatha. See to them." She walked down the spacious hall to Milo's den, where he usually spent time holed up during rainy days. She took a deep breath, then threw open the door and rushed in, arms spread wide in greeting. "My darling," she gasped. "It's so good to be home."

Before she could reach him, Milo stood and spun around to face her, his expression dark and fierce. With measured words, he said, "So, you've decided to leave Preston and come crawling back to me, and I'm supposed to be grateful?"

His words stopped her dead. Her outstretched arms dropped to her sides like broken wings.

"Milo," she gasped, struggling for composure. "Why do you talk like that? Aren't you glad to see me?" This reception had never been fully played out in her mind. Never been imagined.

"Don't take me for a complete fool! You've been living with Preston in London, you slut."

Refusing to let him deter her, she took a tentative step closer, close enough to touch his arm. He pulled it away. "Amanda lied to you, if that's what she told you." Her legs grew weak and began to tremble. "She never liked me, you know. She'd say anything to break us up."

Staring at her, he replied, "Amanda never said one word about it. I had an investigator on your case. He told me every disgusting detail."

"I'm...I'm sorry, darling," she muttered, while searching for an excuse he'd believe. "You know how forceful Preston is. I simply couldn't help myself. But I came to my senses, and I'm home now." She held her breath, dreading his response, and fighting for self-control, every muscle aching with her effort.

"Don't darling me," he spat out. "I'm not your darling, just your meal ticket and credit card. That's all I've ever been to you."

"That's not true, Milo. You really are my darling." Her stomach knotted as she realized he meant what he said.

His brooding eyes darkened further, and his neck turned crimson. With clenched fists, he looked as if he were preparing to hit her. She backed up, but his arms remained at his sides. "Don't do this to us," she pleaded. When he took a step toward her, she shouted, "Don't you dare hit me."

"Don't act the fool." he scoffed. "Pack your things and get out. Agatha can help you." He opened the drawer in the end table beside the sofa, and took out an envelope. "This is all you're going to get out of me," he said, tossing it to the table. "Now, get out."

She stared at the envelope, not wanting to accept the inevitable. "Don't think you can get rid of me like this." she said. Then softening her voice, added, "You know I'll never leave without my harp, and I can't take it in a cab. Anyway, we have to talk this over. Let's not do anything foolish on the spur of the moment." She forced a smile, intending to soften him up. "I do love you, Milo," she added. "Preston doesn't mean this much to me." She snapped her fingers carelessly to give impetus to her words.

"You tramp!" he exploded. "I sent your precious harp to Paris, like you asked, but as you weren't there to get it, I ordered it given to anyone who wants it. That's the end of your damned harp. And the end...of...of... you..." His voice broke, and he looked puzzled, then frightened. He rubbed the left side of his face, then seemed to shrink back. Reeling, he collapsed to the floor, calling out, "Agatha! Agatha!"

Jackie knelt beside him as he lay in a heap on the floor. He looked in agony. She didn't know what to do. Finally, she, too, shouted, "Agatha! Get in here."

Agatha came on the run. "Too much excitement for him, my coming home like this," Jackie explained. "I should have called first. I think he's fainted. Do something for him."

As Agatha grabbed the phone and dialed 911, Jackie pocketed the envelope. Then Agatha kneeled beside Milo. She began brushing away the strands of hair from his forehead. Perspiration beaded on his upper lip, and his breathing seemed shallow.

"You poor dear," Agatha muttered. Then looking up at Jackie, said, "You caused this. You did this to him!" She held Milo's hand in hers. "It's all right, Milo," she said as she patted it. "It's going to be all right. I'll look after you."

Jackie stood watching in disbelief. This...this mere housekeeper loves Milo? What kind of hanky-panky has been going on while I was away? She dropped to the sofa, not knowing which way to turn, or the implications of what she'd just seen. In a daze, she stared at Milo.

Later, when Agatha brought in the medics, she simply stared at them. "Milo? Milo?" she whispered, as they moved him to the stretcher. "What will happen now?" The medics started to carry Milo out. She finally realized what was happening, and said, "I'll go with him."

"I don't think that's wise," Agatha said.

"Mind your own business." Jackie snapped. "I'm in charge here." With heavy feet she followed along. What will this do to me? To our marriage? Suddenly the years seemed to catch up with her, eroding her youth, Milo's middle-age. "It's too soon," she whispered so softly no one could hear. "I'm not ready for this." When the ambulance siren began to wail, tears finally ran down her cheeks.

Preston had called Amanda from his hotel room in Seattle, and after a hard sell, convinced her they had to talk face to face. She fought him all the way, until the last. But she put conditions on it: no talk about Jackie, and they were to meet at a restaurant, not at the house.

He arrived in Kent early, and sat sipping coffee while he anxiously waited. Amanda was late, and his anxiety slowly turned to disappointment. He thought she'd changed her mind. As he arose to go, she came hurrying in, breathless and pale.

"I can't stop," she gasped. "Dad's just been hospitalized."

Preston took her arm. "I'll drive you. Take your car home. I'll follow." He hurried her out, watched her drive away, then followed. When they were on Interstate 5, headed for The Virginia Mason Hospital in Seattle, Preston asked, "What happened?"

"I don't know exactly. Agatha said Dad and Jackie had a row. He ordered her out of the house." She kept wringing her hands, which lay in her lap.

"Did you tell Milo about London?"

"Of course not."

"Then Jackie must have told him." He found it hard to believe Jackie would do so. Not after the fight she'd put up against it.

"Agatha said he'd hired an investigator, who traced her, then told Dad what was going on," Amanda volunteered.

"Where is Jackie now?"

She glanced at him with squinting eyes. "With Dad. Don't worry, you'll get to see her."

"I don't want to see her." Rebuked he didn't say more. He was too ashamed of his past actions.

"I think Agatha loves Dad," Amanda quietly said. "I've thought so for a long time."

She looked straight ahead, and Preston knew she did so to avoid looking at him. "I want you to have the house," he ventured, hoping a change of topic would lighten the mood.

"I don't want it. You move in with your aunts. I'll find a place to live right away."

Shocked, he replied, "Why don't you want it? You know I can't live with them."

Her head shot around to face him. "Why not? They're caring, honorable people. Surely you can get used to that, after what you've been living with."

This rebuke made him swallow hard, though it didn't help. When he cleared his throat, he said, "They're so set in their ways."

"Aren't you?" she shot back, then added, "I don't care what you do. My father is my concern, under the circumstances."

He realized this was not the time to try and reason with her. "We'll be there soon. But we still have to have that talk...about everything." He watched her out of the corner of his eye. She shrugged as if it didn't matter whether they talked or not. Neither spoke again, until they were off the freeway and in the hospital.

Much to Preston's surprise, Agatha waited in the lobby, greeting them with red and worried eyes. She hurried them to the waiting room beside the intensive care unit. Jackie wasn't there, and he sighed with relief.

"Jackie is in with Milo," Agatha volunteered. "He looked awful sick to me. She shouldn't be with him." Then as if thinking of other things, she said, "I should have made him exercise and eat less. You know how he is about his food."

Amanda nodded. "You couldn't have, not with dad. He didn't always behave that way, though."

"I don't think 'Her Highnose' should have gone in to see him. Not after what he said to her. But she's his wife, and they always let them in." She spoke to no one in particular, but the hurt in her voice rang clear. Her sharp features were distorted by what Preston recognized as anger, as she paced back and forth across the room.

Preston watched her rather than look at Amanda's pale face. He thought Agatha probably did love Milo. Why else would she have remained with him all of these years. Especially since Jackie was a demanding, arrogant taskmaster.

Finally Amanda spoke to Agatha. "How was Dad when they brought him in?" Her words came out so soft that Preston could barely hear them.

"White as a sheet. Unable to talk and terrified." She wiped a tear from her cheek. "Never should have married that...that unfaithful wretch." She looked hard at Preston, as if disgust filled her very soul. "I followed the ambulance in. Jackie rode with Milo. When it happened, she acted like her brain had been switched off." Then with a loud scoff, added, "It usually is."

Jackie came out of the intensive care unit, head held high, but her face was streaked with worry lines. She kept wiping her eyes. Amanda stood, but looked beyond her. "Your father is partially paralyzed," Jackie said to Amanda. She avoided looking at Preston and Agatha. "I don't know if he'll recover."

Amanda ignored the statement as she stared at the door Jackie had come out of opened. Then Dr. Wyeth came out, stopping to talk to Amanda. Dr. Wyeth had been Milo's doctor for many years, and knew the family history. He was a short man with only a few strands of gray hair. He smiled when he saw Amanda.

"I'm glad you're here. You can go in to see him for five minutes," he told her, as he took her hand in his. "He talks with difficulty. Partial paralysis in his face, so you do the talking. I'll know more about his condition tomorrow. We'll talk then."

Amanda, keeping her composure, nodded. "Thank you." She immediately went inside. Preston watched as she disappeared from his view. He felt anguish that he couldn't do anything for her.

Amanda found Milo watching the door as she entered and sat down beside the bed. "I know it's hard for you to talk just now," she said, reaching for his hand. "So you let me do the talking. OK?"

He nodded, so she went on. "You knew your health was deteriorating. You should have seen Dr. Wyeth some time ago. I suppose some of the blame is mine. I should have seen you more often. Let's not let that happen again, Dad," she said. Tears began to sting her eyelids, but she managed to blink them away.

"Sor...ry," he managed to say. "Changed... will," he added, struggling to make his mouth work. His left side seemed frozen.

"Don't worry about that now. It isn't important. Only your health." She knew Jackie had caused this, though it probably would have happened sooner or later.

He closed his eyes. "Need...time."

"Yes, you'll need lots of time to heal. And for heaven's sake do as you're told. You never did before, you know." Then thinking to please him, she said, "Do you remember when I was a child? You promised to take me to Alaska on one of those cruises. Remember? Just after Mother died. Before..." She couldn't complete the sentence.

His eyes watered, and he nodded ever so slightly.

"Well then, as soon as you've recovered from this, let's go. By next summer you should be up to it."

His eyes smiled. "Wi..ll," he said again.

Amanda didn't know if his response meant he'd go with her, or whether he referred to the written will. She squeezed his hand. He moved his right hand to cover hers. His watery blue eyes watched her closely. "Sor..ry," he said.

She sat with him until he slept.

Jackie had gone. Preston and Agatha sat alone, space separating them like a vast gulf. Agatha actually leaned away from him, as if to avoid catching whatever might be his ailment.

"How is he?" Agatha asked, jumping to her feet. She chewed at her lower lip anticipating the answer.

"Weak, tired and unable to say much. He seems to be worried about his will." Her head felt dull, her eyes moist, but she managed a smile. "I'm sure he'd like to see you, when he wakes up, Agatha."

"I have to see him," Agatha replied. "Make sure he's all right."

Preston watched, looking sad and apprehensive.

"I don't want to talk about our situation right now, Preston. It can wait a few days, can't it?" She looked at him squarely, no longer trying to avoid his eyes.

Preston nodded.

"Will you take me home now, Preston. I'm terribly tired."

CHAPTER 15

Several days had passed since Preston visited Pauline. As he hadn't returned, she carried each friend down from the attic, apologizing to each as she stood it along her bedroom wall. Preston didn't believe she had friends, but weren't all of these her very best friends? Why even Amanda didn't have that many close friends. Not six. All of her friends would be bridesmaids.

She sat on the bed to talk to them, and each seemed to smile as she spoke its name. They didn't converse much with her during the day, but each night, when it grew dark, they began to advise her, telling her things she'd never known, and making suggestions. They told her of Preston's unhappiness with Amanda, of his longing to have Jackie in his arms, his bed. Sometimes, they would all talk at once, and she'd have to silence them, shout until they were quiet.

She chuckled as she remembered those conversations. Rosemary, with her deep understanding of Pauline, even suggested how to get Jackie and Preston together. The plan worked wonderfully well.

But since then, something dreadful must have happened, causing Preston to return alone. No way did she want him to return to...to... what was her name, that woman who claimed Preston for a husband? Anyway, he'd have to suffer like she had suffered all these years. Tonight she'd consult with her advisers. They were always ready to tell her what to do. She could hardly wait for bedtime.

Walking over, she kissed each one on the cheek. Affection for them overwhelmed her, and she hugged each one again. Standing back to study them, she realized she needed one more, a special one. One she could love even more deeply. She'd talk with someone at her supplier here in town. They'd have exactly what she needed. She could get it quickly that way.

As she looked about her room, she thought of what would happen if Preston arrived unannounced? She could think of no reason for him to come to her bedroom. What would happen if he did? Could she stop him? Her flesh turned cold, and she stood to look out the window. Even if she saw him drive up, she wouldn't have time to take her friends to the hiding room. And if she didn't answer the door, he'd use his key and start looking for her. He'd come up to her room. She'd never be able to prevent it.

Now she began to perspire. She'd have to move. Take bedding, her clothes and all her friends. If she kept a spread on the bed, no one would know anything had changed. Preston would think she'd gone away on a vacation.

Relieved, she sat on the bed again to look at her friends, and when it got dark, she'd tell them of her new plans for their safety.

Amanda reached the hospital early. For three days Milo had been depressed, not only over his condition, but also over Jackie. The quietness of the private room, when she entered, frightened her, until Milo turned to look at her. An unopened newspaper, on the foot of the bed, rustled as he turned over.

"Thanks...for coming," he said. His speech had improved, so Amanda could better understand him.

She took his hand in hers, then said, "You look much better today."

"Don't feel it," he replied, looking grumpy.

"Sure you do. You just won't admit it."

He forced a smile.

She wondered if he was yearning for Jackie. "Has Jackie been in to see you?" Amanda came early, hoping to avoid Jackie, who always slept late.

He shook his head. "Won't see her." He spoke slowly as the words still came with difficulty.

"Why?"

He studied her face, then replied, "Gave orders. Can't come in." After a pause, he added, "London. I know, you see."

"Oh, Dad." She closed her eyes, regretting his knowledge of what had happened, and knowing he'd be deeply hurt.

"Should have guessed...what she was doing. Detective found out." She squeezed his hand again as he added, "Sorry for you."

"I'm fine. Like you, I'll survive this." She knew the worst was behind her though the future looked dim.

"Sorry. My fault."

"Of course not. Only two were responsible. We're not included. Is Jackie still at home?"

"No. Told Agatha...get rid of her."

"Oh, Dad! She can't be expected to do that. Jackie wouldn't pay attention to anything Agatha has to say. After all, Jackie has been mistress of the house for years."

"Said...could manage it," he insisted. "Check it?"

Amanda nodded. "Can I bring anything for you?"

He looked at the door, as if expecting someone to come in any moment. "Agatha...will."

Amanda smiled. Yes, she knew Agatha would take care of him, and he was probably watching for her now. "She's a gem. I hope you pay her well."

He gave a lop-sided grin. "Too good...to lose."

"I've seen a lawyer," she volunteered. "Got things rolling for me."

"Certain... about it?"

She nodded. "I can't trust him again, so what's left?"

"Not much." He looked at the foot of the bed.

"Do you want the paper?" she asked, reaching for it.

"Read it."

She eyed him cautiously. "Read to you?"

He nodded then began to relax as she started to read the front page.

She read until he slept, then she quietly left to check on Jackie. A chore she hated. What would Jackie say, if confronted with an ultimatum to get out? What would her own reaction be to a tirade from Jackie? And there certainly would be one.

When she arrived, no one answered the door, so Amanda used her old key. The house seemed deserted. She checked the kitchen, where Agatha spent most of her time. A freshly baked chocolate cake sat on a plate on the spotless counter top. She called out to Agatha, but got no response. With nervous steps, she climbed the stairs, holding on to the railing for support, a nervous reaction. "Jackie?" she called, expecting to hear from her. If she did, she'd half a mind to leave immediately, rather than face Jackie. I'm a true coward, she thought. Pausing at the top of the stairs, she listened for some movement. None.

With nervous steps, she entered the master suite. Clothes lay helter-skelter on the floor, blouses, skirts, slips, all as discarded trash. Opened drawers gaped at the ceiling, empty of contents. One lay upside-down on the floor, the side split as if Jackie had kicked it.

Amanda sighed with relief. Obviously Agatha had been successful in evicting Jackie. How had she managed it? Amanda dropped to the side of the bed to catch her breath, and let what had happened sink in. She'd have to ask about it when she and Agatha were alone.

As she sat there, memories of her mother flooded her thoughts. Sometimes in the summer, after Milo had gone to work, she'd rush into her mother's bed to talk. They'd planned many a joyous day trip here in the bed. Then after an outing, they'd swim in the pool, and stretch out on the grass in the shade.

Tears came to her eyes. This was the first time she'd been inside this room, for any length of time, since her mother died. It had been kept locked for a year after the death. Then Jackie burst onto the scene and took over like a spreading fungus. But now that horror was gone.

She left the house smiling broadly, and wanting to sing, so she did.

Filled with apprehension, Preston drove to the house he had shared with Amanda. As he parked, pangs of bitter remorse shot through him like sharp quills, each barb leaving a sore trail behind. Even now he couldn't believe he'd been so blinded, so stupid.

He lingered in the car a few moments, trying to collect his thoughts; what he'd say to Amanda. Finally he went to the door, was tempted to use his key, but rang the bell instead. As he waited, he tried to resign himself to what he thought Amanda would say, but he still kept hoping he was wrong.

Molly opened the door. Her face broke into a smile. "Come in," she said. "It's about time we heard from you."

He hugged her. "How are you, Molly?" He kissed her on the cheek before releasing her.

"Oh, I'm fine. And you?" She stepped aside for him to enter, then closed the door.

"How is Hallie? And how do you like this area?" He wondered about Amanda as he looked around. He'd expected her to open the door.

Molly led the way to the living room. "Hallie and Amanda went out for some groceries. Hallie's fine. She's gotten it into her head to live in Seattle. She'd be lost forever there. You know how she roams about without seeing where she's going, or where she's been." She sat on the sofa and motioned for him to sit beside her. "You're back for good?"

He sat on the edge, growing more and more nervous about facing his wife. With a nod, he said, "Seems like years since I've sat here." He looked about again, as if seeing the place for the first time. Everything seemed to have changed. He suddenly remembered the old saying that you can't go back. He winced. "I wish I could redo the past few months."

"Would you do it any differently?"

"I'd never leave here, or Amanda," he said with great emphasis. "Never."

"What a pity you didn't know that beforehand."

He grunted. "I expect Amanda hates me, Lord knows I've given her reason enough."

"I don't think she hates you, but you know, she's a very sensitive person. You knew that before you left here, yet you still hurt her." She watched him closely, squinting.

He could feel her eyes burning on him. "Much more than I ever intended," he said.

Molly frowned. "Why in heaven's earth did you want to?"

He thought for a long time. "I didn't, but the guilt of the betrayal made it impossible to...to keep up the pretense. I had no intention of leaving her, at first. I had no intention of making love to Jackie at the apartment. With too much to drink, things simply got out of hand. Then I thought leaving Amanda would be less destructive to her, than if she accidentally found out. I don't know why, but I couldn't seem to break off the affair." He paused. "Two mistakes that have altered my life drastically, I'm ashamed to admit." A shudder ran along his spine. Some of Jackie's angry words, as they parted, came to him. What had she said about him confiding in Pauline? He couldn't exactly remember, but he'd never confided in Pauline at any time. A tight frown made his forehead ache as he thought about it.

"What's wrong, Preston?" Molly asked.

He blinked to clear his vision, and shook his head to clear his mind. "Nothing I can change."

"Have you tried?"

Depressed further, he replied, "It's useless. She'll never forgive me."

"I won't deny you acted like a jackass, but try to get beyond that." Her lips pursed as she watched him.

What could he say? Looking squarely at her, he replied, "It's not possible. I'll always remember what I've done, and what it's cost me."

A smile slowly softened her features. "I certainly hope you remember, or you'll repeat yourself." Then changing the subject, she said, "You haven't mentioned how I'm dressed. I don't think you ever saw me in anything but overalls."

Looking more closely now, he smiled. "You look great in a dress. How has Hallie taken to feminine clothes? She always said, 'Overalls are the way to go.'"

"Like a silly goose in a corn crib. Gobbling as if there's no tomorrow." She laughed good-naturedly. "She wants to live in Seattle because of all those restaurants. You know how she likes to eat."

"What about you?"

"I like it here in Kent."

"How will you decide?"

She laughed loudly. "A loaded penny. It has two tails, and I always choose tails. Your Uncle Mickey was a machinist, as you probably know. Anyway, he hollowed out one penny, then fitted a thinned, and altered one, into the hollow. Looks quite normal, until you turn it over. If Hallie ever figured it out, she hasn't said so."

Preston laughed. "And that satisfies Hallie?"

"Why not? It's an honest toss."

"You're a scoundrel," Preston said. "You ought to be ashamed of yourself."

"Oh, I am, but I never let it throw me." This time she slapped her knee in merriment. "She'll be like a wet hen, if she ever finds out."

Preston could hear the kitchen door open and close, and realized Amanda had returned. He stood, frozen as if awaiting a death verdict.

CHAPTER 16

Amanda and Hallie unloaded the groceries, then Amanda stood against the door, trying to catch her breath. She'd seen Preston's car in the driveway, and knew what he wanted.

Hallie patted Amanda on the shoulder. "Go get it over with. I'll start lunch. Molly will come out to help me."

With deep trepidation, she entered the living room. Preston stood as if at attention, his back stiff as a ramrod.

Molly said, "Preston came to see you, Amanda. I'll make myself scarce." She left immediately.

"Sit down, Preston," Amanda said. Seeing how nervous he looked eased her own discomfort. She sat opposite, reading the lines of worry on his face. "What is done, is done. Like Humpty-dumpty, the pieces are too small to put together again. I'm sorry, Preston."

"They needn't be." The ridges on his face deepened. "I won't be unfaithful again."

"I never believed you would be at the start, but I misjudged you." The old anger resurfaced. She had thought to be through with it.

"Give me another chance to prove it." His face had reddened as she spoke, and his eyes watered.

She studied him a long time, calming her thoughts. "You've known Jackie for eight years, her habits, her deceits, her excesses. You really have no excuse." She stopped to take a breath. "Preston, I can never forget what you and she did. I'll never again feel secure with you. I'm sorry, but that's how it is. Now, why don't you move back here with your aunts, until they get settled. There is no reason why I can't stay at the business apartment in Seattle for the time being."

"We could both live here, you know, until we get this all settled. I'll use the room in back of the kitchen," he said.

She stood, wanting an end to it. "No. I couldn't do that. If you want to talk about a divorce settlement, that's fine. Failing that, I think you should leave." She felt awkward and uneasy, yet she knew this had to be done. She watched Preston slowly stand, his face ashen, his shoulders drooped.

With a sigh of resignation, he said, "Whatever you want."

She replied, "I'll start packing tomorrow. You can move in on the weekend." Not able to look at his bowed head, she hurried away, confident she had made the right decision.

Before Amanda reached the door, Preston spoke up. "How is Milo?" He asked simply as a delaying tactic, though he was curious about his father-in-law.

She turned. "Dr. Wyeth says he'll be home in no time. The stroke shook him up, a warning of what might come. Only minimal damage, thank goodness. He'll recover, but will have to take it easy for some time."

"I'm thankful it wasn't more serious," he said.

"Me too." She nodded, then left.

Just as Preston reached the front door, Hallie burst into the living room. "My goodness! You certainly weren't going to leave without saying hello to me, were you?" Like her sister, she wore a dress of pale green.

"I'm pressed for time." He turned to her, feeling short of breath, as if he'd been punched.

"Did Molly mention we're house hunting?" She scrutinized his face closely as she waited for a reply.

"She mentioned you like Seattle. Is that where you're looking?" He desperately wanted to get away, seek solitude.

"For goodness sake, do sit down, Preston. You can spare your old aunt a few moments, surely?"

Begrudgingly, he sat on the sofa again, all hope of a quick escape fading.

"I sure do like Seattle, but Molly won't hear of it, silly thing. Can't seem to talk any sense into her."

The look of disdain on her face made him smile. "So, how will you settle it? Split up?" His choice of words rang loudly in his ears, and he regretted them.

"Split up?" she asked in disgust. "Not us. Don't even suggest it. We'll do the usual thing." A faint smile curved the corners of her mouth.

"What's that?"

"Toss for it." The dim smile stretched into a broad grin.

He thought, she doesn't stand a chance.

"Don't look so glum. I haven't told you all of it, yet?"

"Then do," he replied, his own worries fading as they talked. "I'd like to hear it."

"Well," she began. "You remember your Uncle Mickey, don't you?" When he nodded, she continued. "Years ago, he gave me a tricky nickel, both sides are heads. I don't know how he made it, but he did."

Knowing about the penny, Preston couldn't help smiling broadly. "Go on."

Looking like a child bursting to tell a secret, she replied, "Whenever we disagree, we toss for it. But when I'm determined to have my way, for a change, I insist on using my coin, like having an ace up my sleeve. Molly never figured it out, silly thing, though I know about her altered penny." She laughed loudly, her face beaming with pleasure.

"And when you're not determined to have your way?" He couldn't help but laugh with her. "What then?"

"Why heck, I let her use her loaded penny. Works out quite well, really. But don't ever tell her, or she'll be sure as heck to throw a fit. And watching that is frightening, I'll tell you." She laughed again. "Your Uncle Mickey was a smart man. Too bad his mind gave out. You know, Pauline is a lot like him."

Preston's facial muscles tightened as revulsion for what he might have to do made him shiver. "How so?"

She eyed him carefully. "It's like the lights are on, but there's nobody home. Her engine isn't running on all cylinders, nuts and bolts loose somewhere."

He nodded, not knowing what else to do, and dreading what obviously was coming, for he alone could do anything about it. It made him sick to his stomach.

In a surprise change of topic, she asked, "Do you get another chance with Amanda?"

He shook his head. "No, but I had it coming."

"Yes, what a stupid thing you did." She squinted hard. "Preston, I think you ought to know this, maybe it will help. Pauline called us the day you left Amanda, gloating over it, and saying all kinds of things about Amanda that she had no business knowing, even if they were true. I doubt they were in any event?"

"What?" He stood, not understanding how Pauline knew anything at all about his marriage to Amanda.

"That's right. Even told us your lover was Jackie."

"How the hell…" he stopped short. So, that's what Jackie had meant. She and Pauline had been confiding in each other, and Pauline, no doubt, had told lies about him and Amanda. "Damn her!"

"I think she imagined a heck of a lot," Hallie said, "and lied about the rest."

He knew he had no reason to doubt her words. "You think malice is involved."

"Well, one way or the other, the result's the same, isn't it? She helped split up the two of you. If I were you, I'd not tell Amanda what Pauline has done."

"Just what did Pauline tell you?" He found himself sweating, and unbuttoning the top of his sports shirt.

Hallie seemed to be mulling over her words. Finally, she said, "Because I think you should know, I'll tell you some of it. She said Amanda was frigid, dressed and undressed in the closet. You'd never seen her naked. That's why you have no children. She wouldn't even sleep with you, so you'd grown tired of it and turned to Jackie, who willingly supplied your needs. That's for starters. The upshot was that Jackie determined to rescue you." She paused as Preston groaned, his face in his hands. "Why does Pauline hate you so much, Preston? She seems determined to ruin you, one way or another. I'd have her put away. She's a menace to everyone."

Jackie sat in a hotel room, fuming over the events of the past few days. Agatha had informed Jackie she'd rescued all the diaries from the fireplace. The ones Jackie thought she'd burned. Then Agatha had almost bodily thrown Jackie out of the house. "Evicted by a banshee," she muttered as she paced. "Humiliated by a servant! But I'll get even, somehow."

Then she wondered if Agatha really had those diaries? During their battle, she'd managed to get a promise from Agatha not to give them to Milo. In return, Jackie would leave and stay away from the house.

Jackie had consulted an attorney, and learned she'd get half of Milo's estate regardless of what he might think. But she hadn't told the attorney about the diaries. As far as the agreement she'd signed, at Milo's insistence a few years ago, the attorney didn't know how that might affect the settlement. He'd have to see the document first to establish the validity and impact, if any. Then they'd have to talk with Milo and his attorney.

After lashing out at the attorney for not knowing immediately, she'd apologized. After all, he was an extremely handsome man. One should never be angry at the likes of him, and right now she needed a friend, a lover.

In the meantime, Jackie yearned for her harp, and found that using the cut-off tennis racket had become a symbol of defeat. She'd grown to hate the substitute, seldom using it, and felt desperate to get another harp.

She'd visit Milo, butter him up, but Agatha was always hovering over him. The risk was too great. Sixteen years ago she'd married a damned old fool, and she now didn't think the security he gave her had been worth it. Well, she'd show him. No one could make a fool out of her. As for Preston, never before had a lover deserted her, and it damaged her ego, tore away at her confidence, left her uncertain about herself.

In a depressed state, she began to think her age had made the difference with Preston. Had she suddenly become undesirable? She stood. No, she wouldn't allow that to happen. What she needed was a good massage, a facial and a manicure. Perhaps a new dress, using her department store credit cards, would cheer her up. The bankcards were charged up to the hilt. No way would Milo have thought about the department store cards. This would serve him right, the one last fling at his expense.

Yes, a shopping spree lay before her, a real spirit lifter to forget her trifling troubles. After all, the world teemed with available men. All she had to do was look interested, and they'd come easily enough. Hadn't it always been that way?

Within half an hour, Jackie strolled her usual route through her favorite stores. She chose a blue winter coat, shoes, two skirts and several pairs of panty hose. The woman clerk at the counter seemed to take an excessive amount of time to clear the charges. Finally, she said, "I'm sorry, Mrs. Forsythe, but the credit card has been cancelled."

Blood rushed to Jackie's cheeks, and fury to her eyes. "What did you say?"

"Your line of credit had been cancelled; you can't charge..."

"I know what the word means," she snapped at the woman. "You put all this stuff back on the racks, then. I don't really want them anyway." She stomped off, hoping no one who knew her had overheard the conversation. How could Milo treat her so shabbily? Hadn't she given him sixteen years of her life? Kept him breathlessly eager for her? Then he'd treat her like this? "The damned old fool," she said aloud. "Now I'll take him for everything he has. I'll skin the buzzard," she muttered as she left the store.

CHAPTER 17

She had been in the apartment for three days, but Amanda couldn't settle. Even though she'd planned to enroll in fall classes at the university, change her major to Child Development, she couldn't resign herself to attending just yet. There had never been a time in her life where she had been so unsettled. Even sleeping in the bed she knew Preston had shared with Jackie, only caused her to sleep on the sofa the first night, until she realized it didn't matter any more.

The twin aunts had helped her pack, and encouraged her to give second thoughts about divorcing Preston. She'd begun to look upon them as her own family. Then Preston had set her up in the apartment.

Milo had gone home into the care of Agatha's willing hands. She purred around him like a mother cat.

"I'll whip him into shape," Agatha had said on the phone, when Amanda called to ask about Milo.

"Do it slowly," Amanda said. "Let him have an occasional piece of cake."

"With lots of lettuce," Agatha replied.

"He hates that."

"Don't I know it! But don't worry. Jackie isn't here to let him have anything he wants to eat. A little vinegar, a dab of sugar, that's my way. He eats his salads, he gets some lean meat."

Amanda cringed. "And if he doesn't?"

"A big meal of tofu and veggies," Agatha said, with conviction.

"And he takes it?"

"What choice does he have? I don't back down, and he knows it."

"Agatha, you're a gem. Don't ever leave him."

"Don't intend to. It's nice being in charge. I've served enough time to deserve it."

"You certainly have," Amanda agreed.

"He'll be a new man very soon now. Down to size, in more ways than one."

Amanda felt a great deal of gratitude and sympathy for Agatha. She hoped Jackie kept out of it.

Until now, she hadn't much time to think about Brooke and her new family. She called now. When Brooke answered the phone, Amanda could hear children's laughter in the background. "You've got the girls, I hear," she said.

"Yes, and when are you going to get yourself down here? I've told them about you, and every time the door bell rings, they expect to see you walk in."

"Oh, goodness," Amanda exclaimed. "Things got out of hand here for a while. How about this weekend?" Her mood lightened at the sound of Brooke's voice.

"Sure you can spare the time?" Brooke said.

"Time I've got. Loads of it."

"Stay the weekend then."

"Do you have room for me?"

"Sure. If there's a problem, I can bunk you with the housekeeper." She laughed. "I've got bedrooms to spare, and you know it."

"I'll come on Friday then."

"Good. I'll tell Nadine to expect you. You're welcome whatever time you arrive."

A loud burst of laughter sounded in the background. "What's that all about?" Amanda asked.

"There's a game of hide and seek going on. Nadine just found Sally, my eldest, hiding under the kitchen sink. Sally is a real giggler."

"Sounds like fun," Amanda said, wishing she were part of the activities.

"It is. So, I'll see you Friday afternoon. OK?"

"I'll be there." As she hung up, Amanda felt lonely. Life seemed to be moving forward for all but her. She'd come to a dead-end in a maze. The only way out seemed to be backward. Preston had suggested again that she take the house in a divorce settlement. He'd concocted all kinds of excuses as to why she should have it-he might not be in town much, and the wife usually gets the house. But Amanda couldn't take the house from him any more than she could take Milo's from him. The thought brought her up short. Why had that thought run through her mind? The phone rang before she could reason it out.

Pauline cried out, "Jackie's responsible...it's her fault." Her sobs were piteous.

What's she blaming Jackie for? Amanda wondered. How much does Pauline really know? I've never told her a word, and I doubt Preston has. "What's this about Jackie?"

"It's broken."

"What's broken?"

"Her hand."

Confused, Amanda asked, "Jackie's hand is broken?"

"No. Rosemary's hand. You know her."

So it's the mannequin she's referring to, Amanda reasoned.

"And some stranger keeps calling. I can't stop her." The sobbing eased as they talked.

"What stranger. Does she identify herself?"

"I'm not imagining it. She keeps calling, and she broke her hand. I can't fix it alone."

"Just a minute, Pauline. Tell me what happened."

"She fell down the stairs...I think. I didn't see her fall. It's badly broken. She acts like she knows me, when she calls, but I don't know her."

Again Pauline wasn't making sense, so Amanda said, "What can I do to help you, Pauline?"

"Come over, please come help me. I can't mend it."

The plaintive plea touched Amanda. How could she refuse? After all, this is Preston's sister. "Sure. I'll be right over."

When she hung up, she felt she needed a good swift kick herself. Help Pauline glue a hand on a mannequin? My brain must be twisted, too, she thought. At least it won't take long to get there, but Preston ought to be the one going to help.

Pauline sat on the floor, the mannequin beside her. One crumpled hand hung beside the torso. Tears rolled down Pauline's cheeks. "I'm, sorry," she said, as she tried to piece together the broken parts. "But it wasn't my fault. Why didn't you tell me?"

During the past hour, she had ordered Rosemary to tell her when Cole Martin would be coming to her. Rosemary wouldn't speak. Pauline knew Rosemary had the answer, but couldn't wait until dark to get it. She'd hit the mannequin and knocked it down. One hand broke as it crashed to the floor. Then in a fit of temper, she kicked it. She immediately forgot how it happened. Now Pauline's only concern was the shattered hand.

More and more her mind kept slipping in and out of focus. Events often blended one with another, making it impossible to tell the difference between. It happened often, sometimes every few minutes. And soon, Pauline thought, Cole would come to her and stay with her always. She wouldn't be alone anymore.

She sat a long time reveling in her dreams. All remembrances of having called Amanda quickly faded. She talked to herself, to her friends, to Cole, all voices mingling in her quiet bedroom.

When the doorbell rang, she hid behind an old chest. No one had the right to disturb her thoughts, her conversations, and her pleasure. She lay very still.

After several minutes, the bell stopped ringing, and she tearfully crawled over to curl up beside the injured mannequin and sleep.

Amanda drove straight to Preston's office. He would have to do something about Pauline right away, even though she could not think of how it could be discreetly done. Pauline would be furious no matter what. After relating to Preston just what had happened, she waited for his reply. When he hesitated, she said, "Preston! She's got to have help. Do something for her." Angered at his apparent lack of concern, she wanted to lash out at him, but she kicked the leg of an overstuffed chair instead.

"Amanda," he finally said. "She begged me not to ever institutionalize her again."

"When?" she demanded.

"Right after our parents died." He now looked anguished, torn between two evils. "I promised."

She jumped up from the chair. "You're a fool," she spat out. "Knowing what you do. How could you make such a promise?"

"She's my sister," he defended.

Amanda threw up her hands in frustration. "All the more importance to you. Are you going to watch her deteriorate and do nothing about it?" Anger brought her close to tears. "Preston," she begged, "do something to help her. Now!" She began to pace, blinking back the tears, and wondering how to make him understand the importance of getting help quickly. "Preston! She's crying out for help. Give it."

Finally, he said, "I'll see what I can do." He picked up the phone and punched out some numbers, while Amanda paced before the window. Pauline had always been a thorn to Preston, though she never fully understood why. She heard him talking on the phone, but her mind kept trying to sort out Pauline's words. Why had Jackie and Rosemary become one in Pauline's mind? Had Jackie been calling Pauline? If so, why? Nothing made sense.

"The doctor will see Pauline tomorrow," Preston's words cut into Amanda's thoughts.

"What? Oh, but you'll have to get her there. She won't willingly go."

"He'll drop by the house. Talk to her there."

"What if she won't answer the door?"

"She likes him. She'll open it."

"Oh, Preston, you're so silly about her. She called me to come help her, but she didn't open the door when I arrived." She felt a great deal of disgust mixed with anxiety and pity for both of them.

"I'm sure she'll open it," he replied.

She shook her head. As she reached the door, he said, "Wait a moment, Amanda, we still need to talk. How about this weekend?"

"No. I'll be in Portland, visiting Brooke, so it's out of the question." Happy to have an excuse, she was taken back when he said, "That will be fine. I'll drive you. We can talk on the way."

"I'll be staying over Friday and Saturday nights," she said, thinking that would knock a hole in his idea.

"I'll find a motel."

"Not near Brooke's home," she said.

He laughed. "Distance won't make any difference."

Frustrated further, she replied, "I'm leaving at lunch time on Friday."

"I can manage that."

She felt like shouting at him for his persistence. A four-hour drive each way with him filled her with dread. She hated to keep saying no, though she could never say yes to a reconciliation.

Seeing her discomfort, he said, "This isn't about us getting together again. It's about splitting up the assets. That's what we need to talk about. I'll pick you up at noon. Bring a note pad and pencil with you."

She stared at him, then realized the seriousness of his words. "And what about Pauline?"

"I'll take care of whatever needs to be done when I get back," he promised.

Amanda started to leave, but still worried. "Her regular doctor won't be much help. She'll need a specialist."

"Don't worry, I'll take care of it," he again said. "See you Friday."

At the apartment, she felt uneasy. Would Preston actually take care of the problem? Or push it aside?

CHAPTER 18

Milo sat on the patio, a blanket over his lap, the recliner tipped back. The few days at home had given him new life. A sense of relief and calmness permeated his whole body. He hadn't felt this way for years. And with Agatha tending to his every need, he knew he was blessed.

Looking back on his life, he wondered how he could have been so blinded by Jackie, whom he now realized was a very shallow woman. She'd never been a good conversationalist. Her only concerns were for herself and that damned harp. Take those subjects away and she was at a loss for words.

Than he remembered her sexual drive and how he'd enjoyed it for the first few months, before his own urges diminished. That's when Jackie shifted into high gear, and went hunting. What she really needs, he reasoned, is a muscle-bound football hero, panting with raging hormones, and unable to tell an old woman from a spring chicken. And not caring. Milo chuckled as he thought about it.

Then his thoughts turned to his daughter. He wondered how she really coped with the situation dumped on both of them. She always said she was fine, but that was because he had never listened to her, never took the time to understand. When she accused him of not caring about her interests in those formative years, she spoke the truth. He had no right to butt in now, but he worried just the same. His only child and he'd neglected her pitifully. No one to blame but himself. He'd let Jackie set the pace.

Just before Amanda married Preston, and during an argument, she'd said, "He's the opposite of you. Preston is loving and caring and interested in what I do." It had hurt him, knowing she was right. But did she consider Preston her father image? Is that why she married a man ten years older? Can't matter now anyway, he thought.

The day had been chilly, though the sun shone brightly, glinting off the golden maple leaves. A strong wind kept them tumbling to the ground. Fall again, he thought. Years leaping by too fast to keep track of them. How many have I wasted?

"Here's a nice cup of tea," Agatha said, setting the cup on the table beside him. She'd come out quietly, not with heels clicking on the tile as Jackie's always did.

"Where's yours?" he asked. "You know I like company this time of day." And in truth, he'd always enjoyed her company.

"I'll fetch it," she replied. A lop-sided smile put a sparkle in her eyes.

When she rejoined him, they sat quietly for some time, neither feeling the need to talk. Finally Milo said, "In the spring, I'm going to take up swimming again. We can do it together."

She looked at the empty pool for a long time. "Yes, we should. Meanwhile, let's get a treadmill for the winter. See if old Doc. Wyeth will go along. She glanced sideways at him. "You need to do something to get back into shape now."

He grunted his agreement. "What the heck's this God-awful diet supposed to be doing? Rabbit food. That's what it is. Fit only for grazing animals." His words were not harsh, nor meant to be.

She laughed. "Nothing short of drastic measures is gonna help you." She sipped her tea as she straightened the skirt of her blue and white flowered dress.

Milo noted, smiling gently. "Yeah," he commented. "You're much prettier this way. Never did like the way Jackie ordered you to wear a uniform. Far too drab."

Her smile was barely perceptible, but he noted, and wondered again just how she'd managed to get Jackie out of the house. When he came home from the hospital, she'd told him she used brute force. He looked at her now, filled with curiosity. "Come on, tell me how you managed to oust Jackie?"

She lowered her head, looking sheepish. "You better not know," she replied. "Too much bad language." A satisfied smile began at the corners of her mouth.

He roared with laughter. "Any words I haven't heard before?"

She shot him a quick glance. "Not from me, you haven't. No sir!"

"Don't keep calling me sir," he scolded. "Milo will do just fine."

Just then they heard the front door open and slam shut. Agatha stood. "You sit still," she ordered. "I'll handle this." She hurried through the door and out of sight.

Milo tilted his head, hoping to hear the conversation about to occur. After a few moments, Jackie shouted, "I intend to see Milo this time, you old bat." He couldn't hear what Agatha replied, as she never yelled, but he strained to listen anyway.

"Don't you dare touch me. I'll sue you...I said I'll sue you..." Jackie's voice began to fade into the distance, then she screamed, "Milo call your dog off.... Milo! Milo!" The words grew fainter until the front door slammed and the dead bolt-snapped into place. He swallowed, thinking about what could have been.

When Agatha came out to him, she was straightening her hair and smiling. "I told her to see your attorney."

Amazed, he replied, "Is that all? Sounded more like you manhandled her." Of course she hadn't, and he knew it.

She looked at him a moment, then sat down. "How else does one handle the likes of her?" Holding up her index finger, she frowned. "Darn. She made me break a fingernail. I ought to sue her." She bit off the jagged piece of nail.

"So, how did you get her to leave. Throw her out?"

Looking smug, she replied, "I hold the trump cards in this game. She's not likely to come back again."

Not understanding, Milo frowned. "What trump cards? Whose deck are you playing with?"

"Mine. She tilted back her head and roared with laughter. "The ones she unwittingly left for me."

Preston picked up Amanda at 12:30 and they were soon fighting traffic out of Seattle.

"How are Molly and Hallie?" she asked, hoping to keep their conversation light.

He smiled. "Full of the devil. Each one striving to outdo the other. They need a hobby each, and not the same ones."

"Doesn't the gardening keep them busy?" She remembered how busy it kept her.

"Not by a long shot. They both work like dogs all the time. Molly has enough baked goods stashed away to last for months. And Hallie walks around with a duster in one hand and a can of polish in the other."

"That ought to please you." She suddenly felt a sense of loss.

He looked at her for a moment then looked back at the road. "It does please me, but it made me also realize how much of your time the place took. And you did it alone. You never seemed to be doing anything just for yourself. I should have let you finish college, just as my aunts should have been allowed more education. Now they know nothing but work. They seem to have a good time at it, but never do anything just for the fun of it. You and I were no different. We never vacationed, never traveled together, and I encouraged you to quit school. You didn't get your degree because of me. I'm sorry for that."

He seemed genuinely concerned for her. "I thought about attending classes this fall, but I need to settle first. Catch my breath, so to speak." She leaned back, considering her options.

"Once you said you'd change your major, if you could do it over. Do you still plan to do so?"

"I'm not sure what I want to do at this point. I'll probably get a job, until I figure it out."

"In Seattle?"

"I'm not even sure of that."

"It's all my fault. I'm terribly sorry," he again said.

"Perhaps it was to be," she replied. "To get me on the move again. I've been vegetating too long."

"Hardly," he replied, glancing at her again.

"I'm afraid it's so. I thought of little but the house and garden, meals and chores. I didn't even produce a child." Over the years she tried not to think of it, but whenever she heard children's laughter, she'd feel sad and unfulfilled. "I've got to do something to make myself useful."

"You've a good mind; you can do whatever you want."

She looked at him, puzzled. He'd never before spoken of this.

"I'll foot the bill for whatever costs are involved, until you get your degree."

"I hope to get a job first."

"You needn't, but I do need to do this for the both of us, Amanda. Help salve my conscience, a little."

To change the topic, she asked, "What about Pauline? Did you see her?"

"Yes. Once or twice she seemed almost normal, for a few moments." A frown cut across his brow as he spoke. "The house of hers is like a dead thing, moldering around her ears."

"Have you talked to Molly and Hallie about her?"

He nodded before he spoke. "They agree with you, that she needs help."

"Are you going to do anything for her?"

"The doctor has seen her. He'll have a specialist in his office when I take Pauline in to see him on Monday."

Puzzled, Amanda said, "Has Pauline agreed to this?"

"I haven't told her," he replied. "I'll call just before I pick her up."

Amanda closed her eyes, certain Pauline would never agree to go. With a sigh, she said, "Well, I wish you luck."

He replied, "You don't think she'll go?"

"No way."

"I'll think of something. But where does she keep those mannequins you mentioned?"

"In her bedroom. She calls them by name. Says they're her friends."

His head shot around to look at her again. "What?"

"That's right," Amanda assured him.

"In her bedroom, you say? I saw someone in that window with her a while back, when I was leaving her place. A mannequin, do you suppose?"

"Probably, but how can she have kept you in such ignorance of her condition? I don't understand that. She certainly sounded in mental pain when she called me about the broken hand. I'll never understand why she didn't open the door to me." She went on to explain again what had happened.

"If this follows Uncle Mickey's pattern, soon there won't be any real world for her. When Mickey was institutionalized, he never came out again. Nor will Pauline, I fear."

"Why didn't you tell me all of this years ago? Why so secretive?"

After a long pause, he replied, "I never thought it would come to this."

Rain began falling, and he turned on the wipers, then added, "It's just as well we had no children to pass it on to."

She bristled. "You don't like children anyway," she said. She couldn't keep the edge from her voice.

"You can't believe that?" He looked closely at her.

"Why not? You never wanted to talk about it."

"I was afraid to have them for fear of..." He let the words die, and she understood his meaning.

"But you should have told me. I had a right to know." She realized the futility of fussing at him over it now. She changed the subject. "But tell me why Pauline hates you?"

He took a deep breath. Years ago, when she played with dolls, she lost her favorite one, the one she called her 'Baby'. Later, I found it in a puddle at the back of the yard. You can imagine what it looked like. Anyway, she blamed me, said I'd killed her 'Baby'. I laughed at her and she went crazy." He paused for a moment. "Over the years she's never forgiven me for the killing. I had nothing to do with her losing that doll, but it didn't matter to her. Many times I wished I had left the damned thing where I found it, or dug a hole and buried it, and said nothing."

CHAPTER 19

Preston found a motel a mile from Brooke's house. He dropped his case beside the bed and sat down. A headache had bothered him for most of the drive from Seattle, but Brooke had given him some aspirin that helped. She also invited him to come back for dinner. He hadn't intended to accept, but Amanda encouraged him, much to his surprise.

He lay down, thinking to rid himself of the headache before he returned to Brooke's place. He'd met Brooke only a couple of times before, so didn't remember her vitality, her sense of humor. She'd managed to take the afternoon off work, and met them at the door. He immediately liked her and the children. He hadn't stayed long, wanting to give Amanda and Brooke time to visit.

Since his return from London, he'd seen no sign that Amanda would change her mind about a divorce. He thought he'd feel the same, if he were in her place. Still, he hadn't completely given up hope for reconciliation at some future date.

As he lay thinking, Jackie's statement, that had bothered him for weeks, ran through his mind. "You always confided in Pauline," she'd said. But he'd never confided in Pauline. Whatever was she talking about? He remembered Pauline's reaction when she found out about his engagement to Amanda. She accused Amanda of being a streetwalker, amongst other things. He tried to reason with her, but to no avail. Her wild imaginings seemed riveted in her mind. No one could change them.

He turned onto his side, hoping to ease the dull throbbing in his temples. What kind of madness drove his sister into a shadowy world? Where every figment of her imagination took the shape of reality, and every insecurity, a bedeviling phantom? And then there was her obsession with Cole, who couldn't stand the sight of her? Lastly this fascination with her so-called friends, the mannequins.

He sat up. He should have insisted on seeing Pauline's bedroom when he visited her, made some excuse to go up. Amanda and the aunts had seen her clothes and the mannequins, then listened to her tell about her forthcoming marriage, all in her bedroom. He knew deep down he would have to hospitalize Pauline, and he'd dreaded the responsibility ever since his parents died.

He looked at his watch. Just time enough to shower and change before returning to Brooke's place. His mind felt half-numb with worry. He hadn't slept, and his headache lingered.

Rosemary leaned against the wall of the bedroom, her left hand covered with an elastic bandage to hold the crushed pieces in place. None of the other mannequins were present, for they were being kept in the hiding room.

Dejected, Pauline didn't know how to cope. "What should I do?" she begged of Rosemary, who stared blank-faced at her. "I know Cole wants to come to me. I dreamed of him last night, and he told me so. Where is he now? Why hasn't he come? Is he playing games with me? I made arrangements for him to come some time ago. I even paid his way."

The front door bell rang just then. "He's here, Cole's here! He's finally come to live with me," she shouted to Rosemary. She took the stairs two at a time in her rush to open the front door. A strange man stood beside Cole, his blue uniform bright in the afternoon sun. Cole, whose brown eyes gazed lovingly at her, smiled but was speechless. She thanked the deliveryman, who handed her the invoice, and then turned away. She took Cole's arm, pulling him inside to close the door.

Joyously, she guided him up the stairs to her room, into the closet, then up the rickety pull-down steps. She struggled to get him into the attic. With a great deal of puffing, she succeeded. Then she kissed him and rushed back to her room for Rosemary. They could all be together now. One glorious family, the family she'd never had. She introduced Cole all around, to Rosemary, Charlotte, Twilla, Gretchen, Amelia and Clodette. She'd never been so elated in her whole life, never felt like soaring before. Unable to contain herself, she began dancing about the room. Her steps were furtive at first, and often grotesque, but she didn't notice as her feet sent puffs of dust floating about the room, while her friends clapped to some unheard rhythm. Supreme happiness drove her around and around the small room, often with her eyes half closed. All the while, Cole nodded adoringly.

The attic lay in shadows as gloomy as the rest of the house. A single mattress lay bunched in one corner, and an old broken cane-back chair blocked part of the dormer window and pinned the brown, rotting, lace curtain to the wall beneath it. Several old pictures leaned against the walls. One was of her parents in their younger years. Long, dust- laden cobwebs dangled from the peaked ceiling onto the picture. At the head of the stairs sat a basket of silk flowers: yellows, reds, pinks, all faded. A bouquet she'd found by a dumpster down at the apartments two blocks away. She now believed Cole had sent it to her.

A dust-covered mirror at one end of the room returned her dim reflection as she danced by. For her, nothing could spoil this special day, special hour, special moment. Temporarily gone, all memory of her past; the present held her attention completely.

Her new family gathered about her, filled her with contentment and self-esteem. She crooned loudly, and off key, "We'll never be separated. We'll always be together." Finally growing tired, she lay down and slept with Cole at her side.

Preston had returned to Brooke's house with an armload of toys. All three children were excited when he entered bearing gifts. Sally, the oldest, now sat in a rocking chair, cuddling her new doll as she sang softly to it. Her hazel eyes sparkled with pleasure. Candy, just five, rode a tricycle around the room and down the hall, squealing with delight. Her blonde hair hung in curls about her shoulders. Three-year-old Kim held a doll blanket to her face, smiling self-consciously, and watching the adults with inquisitive eyes. Brooke picked her up to hold her and her brightly dressed Raggedy-Ann. They nestled deeply into Brooke's arms.

The three children were completely at home, as if they'd always lived here. Amanda noticed Preston couldn't take his eyes off them. She could hardly believe his pleasure as she watched. He'd have made a wonderful father, she realized.

When Candy tired of the tricycle, Preston, much to Amanda's surprise, got down on his hands and knees to give piggy-back rides around the room and down the hall.

Speechless, Amanda stared. Finally, she whispered to Brooke, "I've never seen this side of him. Not once." She watched fascinated, wondering how this could be.

"Why is that?" Brooke asked.

"I don't know," she replied, baffled.

"Well, perhaps you should think about it awhile." Brooke smiled as she talked, her blue eyes twinkling with pleasure.

Puzzled, Amanda said, "Think about what?"

Preston rounded the corner with Kim on his back. "This kid is a natural rider. She's ready for a horse," he said, pausing to let her get off. "But I'm bushed." Panting, he got to his feet, stretched, then sat down, as Nadine called them to dinner.

During the meal, Amanda studied her husband carefully. He seemed to be right at home with the children, and Brooke. Then while she and Brooke cleaned up the kitchen, he read to the children as they snuggled close to him on the sofa. When Nadine took them up to bed, Preston looked disappointed.

"I envy you those girls," he said to Brooke, as he was going out the door. "Thank you for allowing me to share your weekend."

"You were wonderful with them. They'll remember tonight for a long time," Brooke replied. "You will come in the morning, won't you? They'll be looking for you as soon as they get up."

"I'd like that very much." He took Brooke's hand for a moment, then turned to Amanda. "I'll see you in the morning, my dear." He kissed her on the forehead, then left.

As she watched him go, Amanda felt she had never really known her husband, never understood him.

Later, in the kitchen, Amanda and Brooke drank hot chocolate as they sat at the table talking. "Has Preston accepted your decision to divorce him?" Brooke asked, as she watched Amanda over the rim of her cup.

"I think so. He says he has."

"Is Jackie still in the wings, waiting to nab him?" She lowered her drink to the table as she talked.

"He says not." Amanda put down her cup also. "Why are men like moths where Jackie is concerned? I've never understood that. To me she's...how do I describe it?"

Brooke spoke up. "Oh, but then you know her for her true self, and from the view of another woman. To a man she'd glamorous, desirable, obtainable. Mostly obtainable."

Amanda scoffed, "What fools they are."

"And your father?" Brooke asked, eyebrows raised.

"Him, too. I seldom saw him after the marriage. Jackie met him after work most of the time. I'd go to bed without having seen him the whole day." She thought about it a moment. "It's no wonder I hated her."

"Didn't he check on you when they came home?" Brooke said.

"No. He never cared where I was or what I did. I graduated from high school with honors, but did he care? Forget it. The only concern for both of them was that I kept out of their way."

"You sound bitter, Amanda. You've never sounded that way before." Brooke put her elbows on the table, her chin cupped in her hands. "Why? What's happened that I don't know about?"

"Nothing, it's just that she stole my father, then my husband. If I'd had a son, she'd just as likely try for him, when he grew up."

"Hey," Brooke said. "You're getting morbid." After a moment, she added, "When Preston came into your life, you explained how different he was from your father. That's what drew you to him in the first place, wasn't it?"

"I told you that?" Amanda asked.

Brooke nodded. "When you first started dating him. You always compared him to your father. Don't you remember?"

Amanda leaned back and took a deep breath. "You're right," she admitted.

"Wasn't he the father image you wanted so desperately, but never had, while growing up?"

Amanda didn't want to believe it, but what could she say? "I don't know," she replied, shaking her head. I never saw it that way."

"I did," Brooke insisted. "I've always thought that was the basis of your marriage to him."

CHAPTER 20

"Don't keep bugging me," Amanda shouted, her face flushed and hot. With Preston at the wheel, they were returning to Seattle after the weekend in Portland. "I'm too confused to know right now," she added. Anger and frustration kept her thoughts muddled.

"But it's a simple question," Preston insisted. "Would you have been willing to adopt children?"

"It's not simple to me," she argued. "Why ask about it now, when you know it's too late?"

They'd been arguing over his attention to Brooke's three children. Amanda had told him he made a fool of himself, fawning over them. He'd insisted he genuinely liked them, and enjoyed children, to which she replied, "But not enough for us to have any."

She realized she'd criticized him out of jealousy, but couldn't seem to control herself. "You never suggested adopting, when it was possible."

Preston nodded, but remained silent for a long time. Finally, he said, "If you'd wanted children so desperately, you'd have suggested it yourself, since you surely guessed I didn't want to father any."

"And you should have told me all that right from the start," she snapped.

With quiet conviction, he replied, "Amanda, before we were married, you weren't interested in having children. I asked you and you said you didn't care about them."

Her head snapped around to face him. She opened her mouth to deny it, but the words died on her lips. The forgotten memory hit her full force. She slumped in her seat, shrinking to realize how she'd been in those days, demanding total attention. Or perhaps her own desperate childhood caused her to react that way. Her rebuke of him a few minutes before had been unwarranted. She suddenly couldn't hold back the tears of regret and humiliation. She covered her face with her hands and cried.

"What's the matter, Amanda?" Preston asked, turning to look at her.

"Nothing," she wailed, now sobbing loudly.

He pulled to the side of the road and turned off the motor. She was shaking with convulsive sobs.

"Don't," Preston whispered. He took her in his arms and held her tightly. "Please don't." He pressed her head to his shoulder. "I didn't mean to upset you, darling."

She welcomed the comfort his strong arms gave as she nestled into them. "I'm...sorry," she said. "Forgive me for...being so...so stupid and blind, so uncaring."

"You know I'd forgive you anything."

Jackie hadn't been back to the house since Agatha had thrown her out the last time. She had some regrets over Milo's health, but did not feel responsible for his present condition. He'd always thrown fits of temper to deal with things he didn't like.

Why had she married an old fart in the first place? Only an old crank would cut off her credit cards. She should have waited until Preston came along, prevented his marriage to Amanda.

She often wondered about the two. What was that relationship now? Curious, she called Pauline to find out. After all, Preston might well be available, and it was such fun to be with him.

"Who is this?" Pauline asked, when she answered the phone.

"It's me, Jackie."

"I don't know any Jackie," Pauline countered in a strained and frightened voice.

"You know me. I'm Amanda's stepmother."

After a long pause, Pauline replied, "No, I don't know you. All my friends are here with me." She hung up with a bang in Jackie's ear.

Jackie stared at the receiver, wondering if she'd misdialed the number. Pauline's voice hadn't sounded quite right. She punched it in again.

Pauline lifted the receiver and shouted. "You leave me alone. Don't call me ever again." The phone was slammed down, again banging in Jackie's ear.

"The damned old fool," Jackie said, hanging up the phone. "She's not normal. A few screws loose there." Disgusted, she turned her thoughts to a more pleasant topic, her handsome attorney.

He had a wife, but that never bothered Jackie. Most of her lovers had been married. And like the others, she could tell he might well be happy to have an affair with her. He certainly hadn't objected when she kissed him that last time they met. She'd traced the lines of his cheek and chin with her index finger, while thanking him for his time. Then on an impulse, she raised up on tiptoe and kissed him full on the lips. Though he didn't put his arms around her, she felt his body lean into hers, and she could tell by the expression on his face that he took pleasure in it. She laughed to herself as she ran it though her mind. Next time he'd hold her, she'd see to that. A few tears would cinch it.

Looking down at her hands, she realized she'd have to do something about getting a harp, and soon. The calluses on her fingers would soon be peeling off, then the process of building them again would have to be endured. She thought of the symphony she'd played with, before running off with Preston. They'd never take her back. She'd left just a week before a performance. "Never mind," she told herself with a sigh. "I might even move to London, once this divorce business is settled." Then wide-eyed she added, "Or perhaps Paris. The French men are supposed to be excellent lovers. There's only one way to find out."

Agatha still hadn't told Amanda just how she got rid of Jackie. Sometime she'd have to ask, though it didn't really matter because Milo was in excellent hands now, and his disposition seemed greatly improved. While she dusted the living room of the apartment, the phone rang. Molly was on the other end.

"So, how's it going for you?" Molly asked, her voice cheerful and light.

"Great. It's good to hear from you, Molly," Amanda replied. "Why don't you and Hallie come up tomorrow with Preston. Spend the day with me. I'll show you around town."

"I suppose Hallie would like that. Wait a moment and I'll ask her." After a few moments, Molly said, "She's raring to go. Already gone off to choose which clothes she'll wear." Molly laughed. "Silly goose. Has more clothes now than brains."

"As long as she's happy," Amanda said. "Preston can drop you off here on the way to work."

"I'll be ready, but I'm not sure about my other half. Always running late. Runs her clock an hour late."

"Then Preston can wait for her. Cole will be at the office to run it."

"No. He's on vacation. Be gone for a whole month. But I'll get Hallie out in time, if I have to use a cattle prod." Again she gave a hearty laugh.

"You don't own one," Amanda replied, feeling lighthearted just to know the three would be together tomorrow.

"Well, then a stiff finger in her ribs will have do the trick."

"Be gentle," Amanda cautioned. "She's got a lot of shopping to do tomorrow. More dresses, I'll bet."

"Heaven forbid," Molly gasped. "But you know, Amanda, we need to talk. We'll do that while she has her afternoon nap."

"I don't nap." Hallie countered from a distance. "Tell Amanda to pick a good restaurant, I'm getting tired of your cooking."

Amanda laughed. "I know just the place. A sushi bar."

Molly repeated the words to Hallie.

"Oh, yuck! I'm talking about real food, hearty food, not cat food," Hallie shouted into the phone.

After a good laugh, Amanda assured Molly that she was only teasing. "We'll go the Metropolitan Grill. You can have a thick steak with all the trimmings."

"Now you're talking our language," Molly said. They talked for a few more minutes before hanging up.

Amanda finished dusting, then sat to look out the window, while she thought about the trip home from Portland. She couldn't help it, but she savored the warmth of Preston's arms around her. She wished there had been no need for it to happen, but it did, and it caused her some confusion. No way did she want to believe Brooke's conclusion, that she married Preston for a substitute father. Her feelings while in his arms yesterday weren't those one feels for a father.

She stood to walk around the apartment and think. Preston certainly had traits she'd have admired in her own father, if he'd had them. But surely that wasn't the reason she married Preston. Perhaps the father image had prompted her interest in him, but not after awhile. And why had she denied any interest in having children? She'd actually said that to him. She must have been crazy.

Until she met Preston, she hadn't felt loved since her mother died. She only had Agatha, who was kept far too busy to give much attention to Amanda. Jackie proved to be very demanding. But in the morning, when Jackie lay in bed, Agatha shared some time with Amanda, and then again in the evening before bedtime. For the most part, those were lonely days. What a blessing when Preston entered her life. He gave her his full attention and love every moment they were together. "I couldn't get enough of it," she muttered.

Now she realized Brooke hadn't been far off the mark about the father image. She had married Preston partly because he was the opposite of her father. Now ashamed of herself, she flopped onto the sofa. When did that admiration turn to love? She couldn't pinpoint the time or occasion. She only knew when they returned from a honeymoon in Hawaii, she adored him, couldn't imagine living without him. He'd proved to be an ardent lover, and she'd delighted in that love, even though the marriage might have started out for the wrong reasons. Her love for him now certainly wasn't the love one feels for a father.

As for her father, she visited him frequently now. Agatha smiled more, made jokes, and laughed at what few jokes Milo came up with. The house no longer seemed dismal, no longer held rooms she hated to enter. The perennial gloom had vanished. The last time she'd visited Milo, she heard Agatha singing in the kitchen as she prepared lunch. That hadn't happened since Amanda's mother died so many years ago. Yes, the old house had a new glow about it, life there a new sense of purpose.

After a good rest, Pauline remembered some of her past, though each time the memories grew fewer and dimmer. Proudly she looked about the attic. She and Cole shared her single bed, while all of her friends stood guard along the walls, ready to wake her should an intruder come up the pull-down stairs, though they were pulled up most of the time. She had them installed in her bedroom closet soon after her parents died.

She knew Preston would be fooled by it. She could fool him any time of day.

As she lay half-asleep, a ringing sounded in her head. "Don't be afraid," she comforted her friends as she sat up. "It's just the phone." Without much effort, she had the stairs down and was in her bedroom closet. "Oh, shut up," she complained as she went down to the kitchen. "One of these days I'll pull you right off the wall."

She remembered the strange call she'd had yesterday. The woman claimed to be a friend. "I won't talk to her," she had muttered to herself. "Who is this?" she now demanded, upon answering.

"It's me, Preston. I want to take you out to lunch today."

"I can't," she replied. Then remembering earlier plans to go to Paris, she added, "I'm going to Paris today. The fall fashions are out."

"What?"

"Yes, I'm going to Paris." She immediately hung up as a voice began calling from the attic. "I'm coming, Cole. I promise I'll never leave you," she called out. With that she dashed up to the attic, puffing as she pulled up the stairs after her. "See," she said. "I'll never leave any of you alone. You're all too dear to me. My whole world."

CHAPTER 21

Since yesterday Preston couldn't get his mind off Amanda. As he drove the aunts into Seattle, he kept losing track of what the two women were saying. He'd nod when it seemed appropriate.

Finally, Molly said, "You're not with us, Preston. Are you worried about the office with Cole away?" She turned to look at him.

"Oh, no, not at all. I'm sorry, but my mind keeps wandering. Can't seem to get it focused."

"Amanda?" she asked.

"Who else?" he replied.

"What happened over the weekend, if you don't mind my asking?" Molly, who sat beside him, inclined her head as she watched her nephew.

He glanced at her and smiled. "Nothing much. We got into an argument on the way home, though."

"You call that nothing much?" Hallie scoffed from the back seat. "Sounds like a disaster to me."

"Actually, it wasn't. Got a few things aired out. Should have done it long ago. Seems years since I'd held her."

"You held her while you were fighting?" Hallie asked. "That's a strange sort of fight."

"That's their business," Molly chided, as she turned to face her sister and shake her head.

"I know that," Hallie countered. "Still sounds odd to me. At that rate, you should be fighting with her all the time. Then maybe she'll come home, where she belongs."

"I wish," Preston said, mostly to himself.

"Well, try it," Hallie urged.

Preston thought again of Amanda nestling in his arms, the scent of her perfume, the kisses he placed in her soft hair. Never once did she object. That alone gave him hope. Even if she went through with a divorce, he'd still pursue her, court her. Maybe prevent the divorce. He straightened. Why hadn't he thought of it before? Flowers! "I'll send flowers today," he said, as if the aunts could read his thoughts.

"How will that make for an argument?" Hallie asked.

"Oh, hush up, Hallie," Molly chided. "He's talking sense, you aren't." She removed her sweater and cast it over the back of the seat. For October it seemed too warm, but then she was used to the Montana climate.

"Sure I am," Hallie contradicted. "She'll smell the obvious buttering up for what it is. Besides, flowers are too common for that purpose. Needs something special."

"Rubbish!" Molly replied. "What do you know of courting or love? Nothing!"

Preston smiled. "I appreciate your support, but this is something I have to figure out myself."

"Well, you didn't get into this mess alone. You probably need help to get out of it."

He looked in the rear-view mirror to see Hallie wipe her wrinkled forehead in thought. Her pink dress gave quite a glow to her cheeks. "You two needn't worry about me," he said.

"Need something to exercise our minds. Keep us young don't we, Molly?" She reached over and patted her sister on the shoulder. "Need new interests. At least I do."

With a shrug, Molly said, "Don't mind her. She's a natural-born worry-wart, and as ignorant about love as a fence post in the back pasture."

"Well, then, that makes two of us. Don't mean we can't learn." Then after a pause, Hallie said, "Say, does one of your neighbors happen to be a widower? Don't ever see a woman about the place. I'm talking about the man two doors down."

"That's right. George lost his wife some years ago. I'm surprised he hasn't remarried." He looked in the mirror again. Hallie grinned from ear to ear with mischief twinkling in her eyes.

"Well, now," Hallie began in a light-hearted tone. "A new interest. Maybe I can fix it for him to teach me about romance. I'm not too old to learn, even if Molly is. And he has a wonderful smile."

Molly's head shot around to face Hallie. "No way," she ordered. "Over my dead body."

"Have it your way," Hallie replied, turning to look out the window. "George? I've always loved that name. And the man looks about the right age, give or take ten years."

Jackie came out of the music store as happy as a kid with a new wad of bubble gum. She licked her lips in satisfaction. She'd just purchased a new harp, top of the line, one she'd ordered two weeks before. She used part of the money Milo had tossed at her, the stingy old goat. A thirty-eight string Eclipse harp. And why not? She deserved it. Always had. Then she'd played it in the store before writing the check. She had drawn an audience, which boosted her ego tremendously. As she walked along, she looked at her watch. No need to hurry home as the harp wouldn't be delivered for two days. Her fingers were anxious to stroke the strings again, play the familiar tunes.

She couldn't do much shopping, thanks to the old goat she'd married. She could always demand more money, but it would take some time to wrench it from Milo, the tightwad. Never mind, she consoled herself. Soon I'll have half of Milo's money, a million or so. She didn't, in fact, know just what Milo had accumulated, but it must be quite a lot, and she'd be independently wealthy.

Humming as she walked along, she found it difficult not to look at the clothes in the shop windows. Spending more money after the harp might prove disastrous, until the settlement from Milo. But the thought of wearing last year's clothes depressed her. No way could she be like the timid Amanda, who would wear clothes several years old.

How could Preston have married such a timid mouse? A woman who had never crossed her father, not once. Always did as she was told. How easy it had been to keep her out of the way. Amanda probably said yes to Preston because she didn't know how to say no. But then how does that fit in with what Pauline had told her? After Amanda married Preston, she denied him everything a man wanted. It didn't make much sense, but neither did her complete obedience to Milo.

Poor Preston, to have been saddled with that milquetoast all these years. At the thought of him, she brightened. Could she coax him to take her out to lunch? Nothing ventured, nothing gained, she told herself. And if he isn't back with Amanda, anything might happen. Chuckling softly, she headed for his office, planning for a pleasant lunch and maybe more. After all, he probably lived in the downtown apartment. What wonderful memories it held. And it was close to his office. She almost skipped as she headed for the office.

Amanda and the aunts had spent the morning shopping around Seattle, popping into one shop after another; Pendleton, Nordstrom, I Magnin, and others, looking for lighter winter clothing. The Montana clothing the aunts had couldn't be used here. They'd melt away. With aching feet, Amanda led the way toward the Metropolitan Grill. She'd worn heels and now regretted it. She hadn't thought that the aunts were up to all the walking they'd done.

"Let's stop and see if Preston can join us for lunch," Molly suggested, looking at Amanda sideways. "You said we pass his office on the way." Molly wore comfortable flats, and walked sprightly, as if she'd just started out.

"I'm sure he'll be too busy," Amanda replied.

"Won't hurt to ask," Hallie chimed in. Four plastic packages dangled from her hands. They held new winter dresses she couldn't pass up, and a London Fog raincoat.

Outnumbered, Amanda couldn't refuse, though she didn't want to see Preston just now. "OK, but he'll be too busy." She hoped he would be away with Cole gone. Under pressure, she led the way into the building and onto the elevator. The ride to the sixth floor took only seconds. She stopped and sighed before the office door, keeping her fingers crossed.

"Aren't we going in?" Hallie asked, shoving two packages to rest under her arm.

Amanda opened the door, and the three went inside. Usually a secretary sat in the outer office. Today it was unmanned. Voices sounded in the inner office. "Let's wait in here," she suggested, glad of the extra time. "Give him an opportunity to finish with his client. After the Portland trip, she wasn't sure how she'd greet him. Probably with embarrassment, she thought. She hadn't seen him when the aunts arrived. He'd dropped them off in front of the building.

"At least he hasn't gone out yet," Molly said, as she sat down. Hallie sat beside her sister and kicked off her heels with a sigh. Amanda sat across from her.

Preston's voice became louder, and his words grew angry, though Amanda couldn't make out what he was saying. The second voice she hadn't yet recognized, but it was a woman's.

Then Preston's voice exploded. "That's a lie," he bellowed. "Amanda was never like that."

Amanda straightened her back. She held her breath as she sat on the edge of the chair.

"It is true. Pauline told me all about how she hid in the closet to dress. How she refused you sex." Jackie's voice came through loud and clear. "I felt so sorry for you, you poor dear."

"It's all lies. I never told Pauline anything. Nothing! I never discussed my affairs with her."

Furious, Amanda rushed through the inner door, slamming it against the wall with a bang. She faced her hated stepmother with seething rage. For an instant Jackie's eyes opened wide with amazement.

"What are you doing here?" Amanda demanded. She glanced at Preston, who stood beside the desk pale and drawn.

Jackie immediately regained her composure. "I'm talking to Preston, if you don't mind. I'm only repeating what Pauline told me. No wonder Preston left you for me." Jackie wore a red plaid skirt and waist length navy jacket. Struggling to keep control, Amanda realized just how much she loathed this woman. With measured words she said, "I hate the sight of you. Get out of here."

With a self-assured smile, Jackie replied, "You can't order me about." She leisurely reached for her purse from the top of Preston's desk, opened it and took out a compact to powder her nose.

"Yes, she can. I want you out too, Jackie," Preston said, his voice loud. He looked at Amanda, eyes pleading for her understanding.

"You two aren't together again, are you?" Jackie asked, her voice incredulous. "Not after the love we shared, Preston. I don't believe it."

"Believe what you want," Amanda cut in. "You're crazy enough to believe anything Pauline said. You're crazier than she, only she can't help it."

"I don't know what you're talking about. Do you, my darling?" Jackie reached over the desk to touch his cheek. He pulled away, embarrassed. "I'll see you later," she said.

The aunts, who stood just inside the doorway, now had mouths agape. Hallie blinked as if she couldn't believe this situation had occurred, then she blurted, "Why ever would he want to see a floozy like you again?" Her voice sounded breathy and harsh as her hands went to her hips.

Molly grabbed her arm and pulled her out of the way.

"I don't want to see you again, Jackie. Ever! You're nothing but a plague to me." Preston looked as if all his energy had drained away.

"How dare you," Jackie shouted. "After all I did for you." She shoved the compact into her purse, then tucked it under her arm and started for the door, her lips thin and tight.

Amanda blocked her way. "You say Pauline told you all those lies?"

Jackie smugly answered, "She told me more than I can repeat in a year." Her eyes were dark with hatred for Amanda. "Poor Preston needed to be rescued from you, that's all."

Amanda ignored the reference to Preston. "And you were sucker enough to believe the lies?" Amanda hadn't realized until now, just how crafty Jackie could be.

"They weren't lies. Preston proved it." Jackie insisted. "He couldn't get enough of me, after the way you'd treated him. He reveled in our lovemaking, just as I did."

"You flatter yourself," Preston said, as he continued to lean on the desk for support.

"She certainly does," Amanda agreed. "I'll bet not one of her former lovers looks back on the episodes with pleasure. You must feel like a dirty, old rag, Jackie, tattered from being wrung out too many times, then tossed aside."

Jackie spluttered, "You're both fools," then she took a deep breath. "Jealous! That's what you are. But you needn't be. Preston is a lousy lover. I had to teach him everything."

"You also taught him to lie and cheat. I suppose you're proud of that, too." Amanda stepped aside, now desperate for Jackie to be out of her sight.

As she left, Jackie said, "I'm just happy to see the last of you lot." She marched through the door into the outer office without looking, and bumped into Hallie. "Get out of my way," she snapped.

Hallie, raising now to her full stature, even without shoes, towered over Jackie. Squinting down she said, "Want to make me?"

Jackie looked up. Shocked, she quickly darted around Hallie and scurried out the door, never looking back.

"Deserting the ship, I hope," Hallie called after her.

CHAPTER 22

For several minutes after Jackie left, Amanda couldn't look at Preston. She sat on a chair beside his desk, feeling sick to her stomach, while the aunts remained in the outer office. No one spoke. Finally, Amanda raised her head. "Your aunts would like you to join us for lunch. That's why we came by." She prayed he'd refuse.

"I'm sorry about all this," Preston said. "Jackie simply appeared. I had no idea she was coming, Amanda. I never wanted her here." He sank to the chair at his desk, pale and exhausted.

Ignoring his explanation, she said, "Can you join us for lunch?" She wasn't about to discuss Jackie with the aunts in the outer room. Besides, she didn't know how to handle the situation.

"I can't spare the time," he replied. "But thank you for asking me." He removed a handkerchief from his jacket pocket and dabbed at his forehead.

Amanda stood, then paused to look at him again. "What about Pauline? Did she play a part in all this as Jackie said?"

"I don't know. I really don't." He squinted as if in thought, his eyes sad and moist.

"And what about the doctor? Weren't you taking her to see a specialist?" Though she'd often felt sorry for Pauline, she couldn't muster up any sympathy just now. Not if what she'd overheard proved to be true.

"Pauline said she was off to Paris. Something about new clothes," he replied, "She hung up on me."

"When did she leave?" Amanda needed to confront her sister-in-law, find out the truth, if she could.

"Yesterday, she said."

"When will she be back?"

Preston shook his head. "I don't know. She didn't tell me, just snapped because I'd called her."

"How convenient for her to go away just now."

"I doubt she knew Jackie would come here, Amanda. She doesn't seem that much in touch with reality anymore."

"Nor will she be, until she gets help." Without further comment, Amanda went into the outer office. "Preston can't come," she told the aunts. "So lets be on our way." Without pausing, she continued to the hall door, opened it, and went out, leaving the aunts to silently follow.

The day had started with promise, but turned into a disaster. To cap it off, Preston picked up his aunts at Amanda's apartment, and she barely looked at him. Even the aunts seemed subdued on the drive back to Kent. Molly put together a quick dinner of cold cuts, while Hallie tossed a salad. Neither talked much. Hallie bragged about her new clothes, once, though without the usual enthusiasm.

Then at the table, Hallie finally spoke up. "So what are we going to do about Amanda? She belongs here."

Preston looked up, not able to think of anything that might help him. "What can you suggest? My mind is blank."

"When was the last time you took her on a decent vacation?" Molly asked. She pushed her plate away and leaned her elbows on the table. "Away from here, I mean."

Preston couldn't remember. "Some time ago, I'm ashamed to admit." His head began to ache as he spoke, an ache in sympathy with the pain in his soul.

"Yet you were ready to rush off to London with that floozy." Hallie scoffed her disapproval. "Just what were you thinking?"

"Shush," Molly cautioned.

Preston groaned and shook his head. The French doors in the dining room were open, and a cool breeze ruffled the drapes in front of the doors. The breeze felt wonderful to Preston, as he looked at the deepening twilight.

"That was one horrid trip," Preston finally admitted. "I had my doubts about going, but kept my promise. I wish I could claim temporary insanity instead of stupidity. I've done some stupid things in my life, but that one tops them all."

"Well," Molly said, "Dwelling on the past isn't going to help now. Let's get to the future."

"Is there one?" Dejected, Preston could find nothing in the future to get enthused about.

"Now you cut that out," Hallie ordered. With pursed lips she shook her head. "Think positive, like me." She smiled devilishly at her twin. "With one step at a time, anything is possible."

"But the key is in making the right move," Molly added. "Not just any move."

With a deep sigh, Preston replied, "Look. This is really my problem. Don't get yourselves heated over it. I'll take care of it...when Cole gets back." He had no idea how he'd proceed, but he'd try. At least he'd have more time then to figure it out.

"You aren't procrastinating, are you?" Hallie asked. She looked at her watch, frowned, then pushed back her chair.

Scowling at Hallie, Molly snapped, "You can skip your nightly prowling around the neighborhood for once. "It's your turn to clean the kitchen."

Hallie stood. "Oh, just pile the dishes in the sink, Ma." she said with toss of her hand. "I'll take care of them later." She turned and left the room.

Molly shouted after her, "Well, if you're going to be so stupid as to go out now, at least take a coat. It's going to rain. And if you catch a cold, I'll not nurse you."

"Phooey," Hallie replied, just as the glass doors began to rattle in the mounting wind. "I'll manage, somehow."

The second storm of the fall season brought a foggy mist that settled over everything. Preston finally closed the doors and turned on the lights. "Where is Hallie off to, then?"

"Walks toward that widower's place. She don't use good sense. She's silly. Romance at her age?" She talked as if Hallie were years older, instead of a few minutes younger. "Besides," she scoffed, "Just who would want to marry a sixty-eight year-old spinster?" She paused, and then laughed, adding, "Hallie thinks she's worrying me, but she's not."

Preston smiled. "So, you're letting her dream?"

"Sure," Molly replied with a faint smile. "Don't cost anything. Besides, she's had so little to dream about over the years. I just hope she comes to her senses before she gets hurt."

They talked for a couple of hours, mostly about the family, and the houses the aunts had looked at. Finally Preston realized it was raining rather hard, and Hallie hadn't returned. "How long is Hallie usually gone?" He'd been aware of the nightly walks, but hadn't paid that much attention. Usually, he was wrapped up in his own problems. Anyway, Hallie had started them long before the nights began to close in.

Molly looked at her watch. "She's usually back by now. Silly fool."

"Why does she go in the dark?" He began to worry in earnest. These aunts had become very important to him over the last few weeks.

"Didn't use to be dark at this time a few weeks ago."

Preston stood to pace. "Ten minutes and we go looking for her. It's not safe to be out alone at this hour."

Just then Hallie arrived, approaching the two with a broad smile. She silently unbuttoned her dry coat, ran her fingers through her dry hair and nodded. "I hope you weren't worried."

Wide-eyed, Molly demanded, "How come you aren't drenched? It's raining cats and dogs. Did you spend all this time standing on the front steps?" She looked her sister up and down, a deep scowl forming on her face. "How come?" She then stood, placing her hands on her hips, as if waiting for the explanation from an errant child.

Preston found himself smiling at them, and wondering if Molly had always acted as the mother hen.

"I've learned to dodge the rain drops," Hallie replied. With a quick wave of her hand, she added, "I walk between them." She winked at Preston as she turned and headed into the hall and up the stairs. "I'll be right down to take care of the kitchen," she called out.

As she disappeared, Molly turned to Preston. "Silly old fool. Can't do a thing with her. Sometimes I think her marbles are cracked, or rattling around in that empty space."

Pauline, content in her attic hideaway, periodically raided the kitchen. She'd gather up food in a wicker basket, just as if she'd been shopping, then return to her attic hideaway. Her friends were joyous at her return. She'd give each a piece of candy, as if they were her children. But Cole, like a sulking child, refused to take any. She knew he didn't like to be left upstairs while she went out.

The store of food would last a few days, then she'd go shopping again. Eventually the food in the kitchen would run out, but she didn't think that far ahead.

The last occasion, Cole insisted on going with her. They fought for sometime over it. Eventually, she had to help him down the stairs, then make two trips back. She couldn't help him and carry her basket at the same time. It proved to be a nuisance, but to keep him happy, she obliged.

Soon Rosemary insisted that she, too, be allowed to shop with Pauline and Cole. Then one by one the others demanded the same privileges. Pauline couldn't handle the extra trips up and down, so she had no choice but to refuse to take any of them. That's when Cole began to lie on the bed staring at the ceiling. It pained Pauline, but what else could she do?

She had no concept of time in her murky attic. The autumn weather captured the room, and held it in semi-darkness, and would do so for months. Never once did she worry about the time of day, or even the day itself. They merged one into the other, but with all her friends around her, she didn't care.

Occasionally, the doorbell would ring, which she could barely hear. Always cautioning the friends to be silent, she'd add, "No one will know we're here if we don't talk." But between times, she'd encourage her friends to talk, and they laughed happily. She'd even tell them stories she'd read as a child, thinking they were quite original.

Pauline often changed the mannequins' clothes, shuffling them from one to another, but she always wore her favorite leather skirt and blouse.

Cole wore her old wool bathrobe tied tightly around his waist. He didn't bring any clothes, and she hadn't had time to shop for him.

With Cole staring at the ceiling all the time, Pauline began to feel sorry for herself. After all, hadn't she done her best for the friends? One day in desperation, she jumped up and told her friends to dance. She took their hands and danced them around the room to some unheard music. All except Cole participated.

She now began to fear he would leave her, and if he did, would all the others? The thought terrified her. She'd never live alone again. In desperation, she rushed around the room kissing them all, which seemed to please them, except for Cole. No matter how many kisses she placed on his mouth, he never blinked, nor responded, and she ached to be hugged.

Knowing his upset stemmed back to her refusing to take him shopping with her, she said. "Don't worry, Cole. I'll never leave you again, not ever. No matter how hungry we get, I won't go shopping any more."

CHAPTER 23

"I need to talk to you," Amanda was saying to Brooke over the phone. She stood against the wall, brushing a piece of lint from her pale blue pants suit. "Can I come tomorrow for a day or two?"

"Sure. What's up?"

"I'd rather not go into it over the phone," Amanda replied. "Will it be all right if I come tomorrow afternoon?"

"Of course, but I do have to work Fridays."

"That's fine. I'll stay and help Nadine with the kids on Friday." Today was Wednesday, and she was anxious to be away in case Preston called.

"This anything to do with Preston?"

With a heavy sigh, Amanda replied, "Every bit. Now he's sending flowers...and candy." Disturbed by the implications of his gifts, she nevertheless felt a deep pleasure each time they arrived.

"He's wooing you again," Brooke said with a laugh.

"I know that. But what do I do about it? That's the problem." Amanda, feeling close to tears, closed her eyes a moment.

Brooke burst into laughter. "Do? Enjoy the candy, smell the flowers. Savor the attention."

"Be serious, Brooke," Amanda scolded.

"You think I'm not? Look on the bright side-he isn't sending them to Jackie."

Repulsed by the thought, she shook her head. "But I've told him I won't take him back." She paused. "I thought he believed me."

"Obviously not."

"What should I do now? That's the problem."

"Come on down and we'll put our heads together."

"Tomorrow then?"

"Sure." After a slight pause, Brooke asked, "Is Preston coming with you?" Her voice had the hint of soft laughter in it.

"He is not!"

"Just asking," Brooke replied, laughter still in her voice. "See you tomorrow."

After she hung up, Amanda sat before the living room window, her eyes closed. Why had Brooke found the situation amusing? She supposed Pauline wouldn't find it amusing.

Had she actually told those lies to Jackie, or did Jackie make them up on the spur of the moment? A ruse to shake the blame from herself? She wished Pauline weren't in France just now.

She stood and paced about the small room, with its ecru carpet and pale blue furniture. The vase of roses sat on the oak end table beside the sofa. Pausing before them, she took the time to inhale the aroma, which caused a large lump to form in her throat. Before she could stop herself, she began to cry, though she couldn't think why. "Damn," she muttered. "Why does he keep pestering me, upsetting me? Making me cry? If this is Pauline's fault, I'll strangle her when she gets back, and Preston, and Jackie. Damn the whole lot."

Milo's attorney had just left, so Milo called out to Agatha, waited a moment, then called again rather loudly.

She came hurrying into the library, where he sat calmly waiting. She eyed him up and down, then said, "What's wrong?" She took a deep breath, as if she had been running.

Milo replied, "I need a drink." Jackie had angered him with her demands. He now hated her, and that anger reflected in his voice for some time after his own attorney left.

A hard frown covered Agatha's face. "The sherry is in the credenza, not three feet from your elbow," she said rather sharply.

"Don't be angry," he said, lowering his eyes.

Agatha, who had started for the door, turned to face him again. Her bright-pink, flowered dress gave a rosy glow to her cheeks. "Look, Milo, we go through this every time your attorney comes. You get angry about something and start yelling the moment he's out of sight. Normally you'd have fixed yourself a drink, not called me from the other end of the house. You no longer need a nursemaid."

In truth, he had almost recovered from the stroke, at least as far as he probably would. "Sorry," he said. "I didn't mean to upset you."

"Then why do it?" She turned to leave.

"Wait a moment," he pleaded. "Sit down and talk to me. I need your advice, I guess."

"Why not just say it in the first place, and quit the hollering." She sat down opposite him. "Jackie again?"

"Hell, yes. She wants half of everything I own, and monthly alimony."

Agatha's back stiffened as a frown crept across her face. "Oh, does she? Well, we'll see about that." With a wicked smile, she nodded. "Is that the only problem?"

"Isn't that enough?"

"Sure, but I can handle it."

He felt the beginnings of a smile curve his lips, and his anger left. "You amaze me. You boss me about like a four-star general, make me eat rabbit food as if we're up to our necks in it, deny me my favorite chocolate cake, and here I am liking it. I've lost thirty pounds, thanks to you. And I'm feeling better than I have in years. Now you say you can solve my problems with Jackie. How?"

"Not altogether solve," Agatha refuted. "Just lop some off the size of her demands." She stood, leaned over him and quickly kissed his forehead.

As she went out the door he called out, "You'll still marry me when this is all finished, won't you?"

Without missing a step, she answered over her shoulder, "Not if you keep yelling at me. Change your ways, and I'll keep thinking about it."

Jackie slammed down the phone, furious with herself as well as Agatha, dear, reliable Agatha-the guardian of the town's tightwad. "Well, I'll never go back to Milo if he crawls to me on his fat belly," she muttered. "How dare that lowly housekeeper threaten to use those diaries against me? To hand over my personal diaries to Milo, if I didn't lower my divorce demands." Agatha had demanded Jackie take one lump settlement. A reasonable settlement, or else.

Furious, she sat down to think. Just how damaging could those diaries be? Should she confess to her attorney, see what his thoughts were on the topic? But then he wouldn't respect her, and he'd not want to become involved with her. She'd better keep quiet.

Over the past week or so, Jackie had played her new harp, with several hours a day of religious music filling her apartment. God would certainly overlook some of her sins for such devotion. God, but not the courts of law.

She tried to recall the lovers she'd taken over the past years. Only a few names came to mind. There must be a couple of dozen. Maybe more. Had she named them in the diaries? She had, and to her regret, she realized in some cases, she'd added events and description far in excess of the actual happenings simply for the sake of a juicy diary, and to pretend how exciting she found it all. What ecstasy she hadn't experienced in the relationships, she made up. She didn't know why she'd done that, except that it made terribly good reading when she felt blue.

Each new love soon became dull. Except Preston. Why had she met him so late in her life, after Amanda had snagged him? Why, she'd have been willing to have children with Preston, if she'd met him soon enough. But he had returned to Amanda, as each lover had returned to his wife, after the affair cooled. She couldn't remember having had an unmarried lover.

With her mind jumbled and a heavy headache, she refused to think on it further, leaving the apartment for a walk and some fresh air. She'd been doing a lot of reminiscing of late. Still, she couldn't decide what to do about the diaries. With only harp playing to sustain her, she didn't think she could support herself. Didn't even want to.

How much money did she need to live comfortably? A financial adviser could tell her. And would Milo accept such a figure? Maybe she should try to see him again. On second thought, the attorney had advised against it. But why should she bow to Agatha's demands? What were the options?

Should she simply let Agatha give the diaries to the old goat? Let him sizzle like over-cooked bacon? No, that wasn't a good idea. He'd take her to court, smear her name all over Seattle. She stopped walking. "The old witch," she muttered of Agatha. "Milo deserves her. They ought to make a great pair." Then thinking on how heavy Milo had grown over the years, she added, "A blimp tethered to a shoe string." With that, she started to laugh. Yes a perfect pair of tightwads.

Pauline's mind had cleared somewhat, as she sat talking to Cole, explaining how she'd tricked Preston into believing she'd gone to Paris, though she could no longer think why she'd go there. The attic lay in total darkness. With the exception of Pauline and Cole, the others were supposedly asleep. The two talked cheerfully, Cole occasionally laughing.

"He'll never guess," Pauline added, speaking of Preston.

"Don't be too sure," Cole replied, as he lay on the bed still and straight.

It amazed Pauline to see he could lie perfectly still, as if he were too stiff to move. She couldn't do it, couldn't keep still more than a few minutes at a time. Even now she grew restless and stood to straighten her legs, legs that needed exercise but got less and less every day, growing weaker all the time.

When she lay down again, her mind had lost its trend of thought. "What were we talking about?" she asked Cole.

"Food."

"Food?" She hadn't remembered.

"I'm hungry," Cole said. "Terribly hungry."

"So am I," Rosemary chimed in. "I want something to eat." The talking had evidently awakened her.

"I can't give you anything," Pauline replied. "We're out of food."

"Then go shopping," Rosemary demanded. "And get some treats while you're at it. We haven't had any chocolates for days. And you know how we love them."

"You know I can't do that," Pauline protested. "I can't take all of you." Tears of frustration began to sting behind her eyelids.

"Then just take me," Rosemary said. "I'll help you."

Cole immediately sat up. "If you go, I go. I'm far more important than you."

"That's what you think. I've been here taking care of Pauline for months. You've never taken care of her. Never lifted so much as an eyebrow to help or advise her. All you do is laze about."

"What about the rest of us?" Twilla demanded. Usually quiet, she stamped her foot on the floor, which made the floor boards spring.

"I'm the most loved. The rest of you don't count," Rosemary said, her voice raspy with impatience.

Cole sprang from the bed, shouting, "No you're not. I'm the only one here of importance."

Rosemary and Twilla began to argue with Cole. "Be quiet," Pauline ordered. "Everyone outside will be able to hear you. Is that what you want? You'll be taken away from me and put in an institution. You won't like it there one bit. I certainly didn't."

"It's night-time," Twilla defied. "So I can shout all I want. No one will hear me."

"And so can I," Charlotte cut in. "And Gretchen, Amelia and Clodette. Can't we girls?"

"Just try us," they said in unison.

"So get us some food, or we'll all shout the roof in," Twilla threatened.

Pauline heard shuffling feet scraping like sandpaper along the floor. She covered her face with her hands. They'll hurt me, if I don't get some food for them, she thought. What can I do?

Cole shoved Pauline onto the floor and stood over her. "You promised never to leave me again," he snapped. "You know you promised. I'll leave here, if you go without me. You'll never see me again."

Shrill screams suddenly filled the room. Pauline jumped up, shouting, "Be quiet, and I'll see what I can do when it gets light outside."

The screams continued. Nothing she could say quieted her friends. Angered, she rushed about the room slapping each one on the face, but the howling grew louder. Finally, with her head aching and her stomach cramping, she lay down on the bed beside Cole, who lay outstretched on his back.

With a pillow over her head, it seemed to Pauline that the screams didn't diminish at all. Soon the hurt in her stomach became so painful she couldn't hear her tormentors any longer. Finally sleep came in a troubling dream. The image of a giant slice of bread drifted around in her mind, then a jar of jam and a cube of butter. Frantically, she caught the bread and was able to slather butter and jam all over it. But when she opened her mouth to take a bite, it had vanished.

CHAPTER 24

The chilling October winds blew in fitful gusts, making the trees moan in rebellion. Rose petals lay scattered across the lawn and bunched beneath the shrubs at the edge. Huge drops of rain pelted the garden path, jumping on impact, then settling in the puddles of water at the edges. Preston stood looking out from the patio doors, feeling dejected.

"Doesn't this ever stop?" asked Hallie, who sat on the sofa watching her nephew.

"This is nothing like your incessant snows in Montana," he objected. "It's wet out there, but it won't freeze your toes off."

"But it's so depressing," Molly replied.

The downpour reminded Preston of the night he foolishly stayed in Seattle with Jackie. He hated himself for that action. He had lied to Amanda as well. Jeopardized his whole life for a few words of sympathy from Jackie. He took a deep, shuddering breath.

"Does it rain like this all winter?" Molly asked, as she joined Preston at the window.

"Not this heavy, usually," he replied, bringing his mood back to the present. "Mostly we get fog and drizzle." Forcing a smile, he added, "Stay out in it too long and you begin to grow moss on your head."

Hallie laughed. “Sounds wonderful. Does it grow at night, too?”

Molly turned to face her sister, who looked at her watch. “You won’t go out in this weather,” she ordered.

“Don’t intend to. I’ll walk one of the malls in Seattle tomorrow.” Without looking at Molly, she added, “With George.”

Molly gasped. “You’ll what?”

Amused, Preston turned to look at Molly. He smiled as he saw her mouth agape.

Finally, Hallie looked up. “That’s right. He’ll be here for me at ten tomorrow. We intend to spend the day in Seattle.” While Molly stood staring, Hallie added, “Arm in arm.”

“That’s wonderful,” Preston volunteered quickly, hoping to delay any comments from Molly. “He’s a fine man.” He sat down opposite Hallie, leaning toward her and thinking it’s time she had a life of her own.

“He’s too short for you,” Molly blurted, “Don’t be a fool.” Pouting, she added, “Probably younger than you as well.”

“Oh, he’s all of that,” Hallie agreed. “Makes it more exciting, doesn’t it? But we’re...what do you call it? Oh yes, kindred spirits. We see eye to eye.”

“How can you, when he’s a foot shorter?” Molly snorted.

“Six inches,” Hallie corrected. “And there are such things as elevator shoes, and barring that, I can still bend, though I don’t know why it should bother you.”

“It doesn’t bother me, but it soon will him,” Molly charged, her face pale and strained.

Preston, confused by Molly’s attitude, felt sorry for Hallie. “Look, Molly,” he began. “They’re only going into Seattle. No harm in that.”

Molly turned, then sat down beside Hallie, patting her hand as she talked. “But don’t you see? She’ll just be getting silly ideas. Ideas best left to the young.” Then as if to douse any future plans Hallie might have, she turned to Preston and added, “No way will she make a good wife. Can’t cook worth two hoots.”

Hallie jerked her hand away. “Says you!” She jumped to her feet, facing her twin. “The green-eyed monkey is on your shoulder again, baring its teeth.” After a pause, she relented. “Sorry, Molly, I didn’t mean that.”

"Nor did I," Molly replied. "But...don't let yourself...get too involved. I don't want you hurt again." Molly lowered her face to her hands and sat hunched over.

Preston ached for them both, knowing how deeply they loved each other. "Look," he said, forcing a smile. "Let's not let the dismal weather get to us. Put your coats on, we're going to the movies."

Within minutes, all were headed into town. Preston wondered about Amanda, as he drove through the rain. Was she sitting alone in the apartment? Should he call her, invite her to join them? Would she even consider it? Suddenly he thought of that first night with Jackie in the apartment. He cringed. Would the memory of that mistake ever fade from his mind? He'd give almost anything to get rid of it.

"Is there a good jeweler in town?" Hallie, who sat beside Preston, asked. "A trustworthy one?"

Preston's head snapped around to look at her. "Sure," he replied. "Several. Why?" He hadn't needed to ask, but didn't know what else to say. If Hallie were to marry George, Molly would be totally lost. She'd looked after Hallie all her life. What would she do then? Interfere in Hallie's affairs? No, he would not allow that, but would have to find some other interest for Molly. A woman with her talents ought to find something to occupy her time. She keeps a spotless house, cooks like a trained chef, and is excellent company. Why I'll hire her as my housekeeper. Then if Amanda comes back home, she can continue her education, or whatever else she wants.

Amanda found the trip to Portland tiring. More than anything, she wanted to sleep. She hadn't done much of it lately. Half the nights were passed pacing the floor. Should she or shouldn't she? One minute one way, the next another.

Her mind had been made up...once. Why had doubts crept in? Wasn't she capable of making a rational decision? She could not consult Preston, as she usually did. He had always been her able and willing adviser. Yes, this decision would have to be hers alone. "Am I better off with or without Preston?" she muttered. No answer came.

She took a deep breath as she pulled up in front of Brooke's house at six-thirty. Darkness had settled, and the house lights sent bright rays across the grass in front. It had rained earlier, and the grasses were heavy with sparkling diamonds. She sat for a moment admiring the spectacle.

Sally, the eldest of the girls, opened the front door and waved, motioning for Amanda to come in. "Hurry," she yelled.

Amanda got out, grabbed her backpack, locked the car and rushed for the door.

"I just knew it was you," Sally said, her face beaming.

"Oh, did you?" Amanda dropped her pack just inside the door, knelt and gave Sally a big bear hug. "You've grown since I saw you last."

Sally, still smiling, replied, "Not much, but I sure want to be tall like Brooke."

Amanda looked up as Brooke came down the hall. "I can see what you mean," she said. "Looks like a beautiful, tall willow, doesn't she?"

Sally giggled, then picked up Amanda's pack. "I'll take it up to your room."

Surprised, Amanda said, "That's very kind of you."

Again Sally giggled, then headed up the stairs.

As Amanda gained her feet, Brooke, the dimples in her cheeks very prominent, said, "So, you made it just in time for dinner. How was the trip?" She hugged Amanda, then kissed her on the cheek.

"Boring. I'd like to take Sally back with me to liven up the trip."

With a shake of the head, Brooke replied, "Not on your life, my friend. I need every one of the girls. Besides, Nadine would shake you out of your skin if you even tried. You'll have to get your own girls."

As the two walked into the living room, Candy and Kim, who were hiding against the wall beside the doorway, jumped out and yelled, "Boo!"

Amanda, feigning shock, jumped, then put her hand over her heart and breathlessly said, "You scared the daylights out of me."

Both girls doubled over with laughter. Amanda grabbed both in a bear hug. They writhed with laughter in her arms.

Later, when dinner was finished and the girls tucked into bed, Amanda and Brooke sat on the sofa to talk. Pensive now, Amanda didn't know where to start, with her unsteady, wavering emotions, or with Preston's obvious courting? Or with her growing desire to get at Pauline?

Brooke watched Amanda carefully for several minutes. Finally, she said, "So? Has the problem evaporated on the trip down?" Her bright blue eyes held a hint of amusement.

With a mock smile, Amanda replied, "That's not it, exactly. I was absolutely sure about a divorce... for some months. But now I'm not so sure."

"The flowers and candy? Or second thoughts?"

"I don't think it's the attention. That's not what I wanted."

Looking puzzled, Brooke asked, "What did you want?"

With a shrug, she replied, "That's just it. Now I don't know." Preston's first passionate kiss came to mind. She could feel it on her lips even yet. She rubbed her hand over her mouth and closed her eyes. That kiss had sent shivers racing down her spine. What had gone wrong? "Once, I thought I knew," she added.

"Do you still love him?"

She leaned her head back onto the sofa, looking at the ceiling as she thought. "I hate what he did, to himself and to me. How can I love him now?" Her throat grew tight as she swallowed back tears.

"You can hate his actions all you want, but that doesn't preclude your loving him."

"It should," Amanda protested. "It certainly should."

"Is that what you think, or what you feel?"

She turned to look at Brooke. "They're one and the same."

"Wrong."

Amanda said, "Isn't that splitting hairs?"

With a shake of her head, Brooke replied, "Only if you think dawn and sunrise are the same."

"But..." The words died unsaid. She knew her friend had a point.

"How much of your life are you willing to spend without Preston? At age twenty-eight, you've a long, lonely way to go, unless you find someone to take his place. That's possible, of course, even probable. But can you forget Preston? Only a couple of years ago, you told me he was all you've ever dreamed a husband could be."

"I remember, but that was before..."

"If you can't forgive him, you'd better let go."

Amanda turned to look out the window at her back. The street light on the corner had dimmed. Drifting fog blocked out some of the usually bright glow.

Brooke, following Amanda's gaze, said, "You wouldn't get rid of that street light just because it's temporarily dimmed, you know. Nor would you get rid of a dress because of a spot that can be washed out."

"Or a husband who strayed?" Amanda replied.

"Not if you still love him."

"That's the real question, then, isn't it?"

Brooke nodded. "You guessed it. And only you can make that decision."

"But my emotions are on a roller-coaster," Amanda protested.

"Then write down the pro's and con's of it all. Take a logical step to clear your mind. And don't let incidentals sidetrack you. You either still love him, or you don't. Get yourself straight on that point, then you'll know what to do." She paused. "Now, with that behind us, let's have a game of Scrabble. Brighten up the mood."

CHAPTER 25

Milo had offered Jackie a lump sum of money. A generous lump sum. Her attorney advised, "Hold out for more. You're entitled to half of the estate, minimum. This offer doesn't begin to meet that."

Jackie had just seen a financial adviser, and the amount Milo offered would more than adequately meet her needs, especially if the offer included some of his stocks and bonds, an income for life.

She had decided to move to Europe, having considered Spain and Italy, but had come to the conclusion she would be better off in Paris, where the language would not be a problem for her. She'd find some nice, quiet place, close to Paris. Someplace where no eyebrows would be raised when she took another lover. She could live economically, if she had to stretch out her funds, yet could still live comfortably. And from Paris she could always hop across to London from time to time, though she would never again stay at the Savoy. The memories of her stay with Preston still burned in her mind. They were glorious days, before Amanda showed up.

As she walked along the street, her past came to mind. Of all her lovers, there was never, nor could there be another Preston. Perhaps she could find a gentle, easy-going companion in France to share her life.

She felt herself lucky to avoid the scandal of a divorce, since Milo most certainly would expose her activities if he had to. She'd never had many friends, only those in the symphony. None of them knew her as anything but kind and talented. It was important to her that they remember her that way.

For some months now, she had realized her sexual passions had begun to wane. Her mind no longer dwelt on it, though those desires were by no means dead. She sighed as she thought about it, wondering what might have been if Preston had stayed with her.

Before going back to her apartment, she drove to a nearby grocery store. She intended to replenish her scant supply of food. She didn't intend to buy much. Just as soon as the money was in her hands, the divorce papers signed, she'd be on her way to Paris.

After locking her car, she turned in time to see Pauline drive into a parking space not far away. She stopped walking, frowning at what she saw in Pauline's car. Who was that man in the back seat? Why the sly old thing has a lover. Acting afraid of her shadow, but having a lover, who appeared to be a lazy loafer. The man sat sprawled on the back seat, his head against the window.

Intrigued, Jackie watched as Pauline got out of the car, leaned forward and spoke to the man. After a moment, she closed the door and headed into the store. She seemed a bit unsteady on her feet.

Too curious to ignore the situation, Jackie sauntered up to Pauline's car, expecting to speak to the man, and get a good look at him. The first thing she noted was the old, ratty bathrobe he wore. She gasped then hurried away into the store. Pauline had a mannequin in the back seat of her car. The hairpiece he wore covered some of his forehead, having slipped on the ride to the store. And Pauline had talked to it! "She's a real nut case," Jackie muttered.

Inside the store, Jackie spotted Pauline at the candy counter; curiosity pulled her along to leisurely follow. Pauline filled two plastic bags with candies, mostly chocolates. She seemed to be leaning on the cart a great deal. From there she went to the deli section, then the bakery, where she placed two bags of sweet rolls in the cart.

Jackie chuckled to herself as she watched Pauline's actions. She looks as if the devil himself pressured her. She's buying enough for a dozen people. Is she now running a boarding house for mannequins?

After Pauline left the dairy case, she went to the check-out counter. Lagging behind, Jackie pretended to look at the magazines. She hadn't taken a cart for her own shopping, so enthralled was she in Pauline's actions. As Pauline pushed her cart out of the store to her car, Jackie stood just inside the sliding doors to watch.

Pauline abruptly stopped beside the car, then looked about as if terrified. The mannequin was gone. Her hands flew up to her mouth, and she began to cry. Opening the door, she tossed her groceries helter-skelter onto the back seat, slammed the door, and then ran around the parking lot searching for the lost mannequin. Frantically, she ran about, almost falling, as she looked from one car to another. Her legs were wobbly, her steps unsure.

Jackie, caught up in Pauline's obvious distress, began to feel sorry for her. Should she go to her, try to calm her down? Before she could decide, Pauline returned to her car, her face screwed up in hopeless anguish. She got inside the car and drove away. Others had noticed the strange behavior and Pauline's hasty departure, which made Jackie uneasy. She knew she should have gone to help. After all, she'd known Pauline for some years.

Jackie remembered her last conversation with Pauline, and thought she was crazy then. Shrugging, she went inside to do her own shopping, but still felt uneasy. What could she have done? Probably nothing. Oh, let Preston sort it out, she thought.

Pauline stashed groceries in the refrigerator, then took the rest to her bedroom closet, ready to take them up the ladder. Tears still blurred her vision, and involuntary sobs wracked her body. Cole had left her, even though he'd promised to stay with her forever. Had he gone back to the office? Should she call him? No. She'd wait for his return. He would come back, she just knew he would.

As she pulled down the stairs, her friends started to clamor for candy. "What kind of candy did you bring?" they called out. "Chocolates? Hurry, hurry."

Pauline carried up one sack of groceries then went down for another. All the while, Rosemary kept yelling, "Hurry up. We can't wait much longer." Pauline had usually been prompt about the supply of candy, giving each some before she did anything else.

She dropped the last bag on the floor in front of Rosemary. "If you're in such a hurry, help yourself. I'm too tired right now." Her head ached, and she felt sick all over. Too exhausted to stand up any longer, she rolled onto the bed, crying loudly, and panting from the exertion of climbing the stairs three times.

"Where's Cole?" Rosemary demanded. "What have you done with him?"

"Oh, shut up!" Pauline snapped, her usually kind voice harsh with annoyance.

"He's left you, hasn't he?" Twilla asked, her voice oozing with satisfaction. "Well, you paid too much attention to him. You spoiled him. Serves you right."

Pauline rose up to face Twilla. "You're next, if I have any more from you."

All the mannequins gasped, but none spoke.

Face down on the bed again, Pauline tried to think. Where has Cole gone? To the office, or home? The ache in her empty stomach brought her mind back to the groceries. Slowly, she went to the bags and removed a package of butter-horns. "If the rest of you want anything, help yourselves." Her mind began picturing Cole at his office desk, as she tasted the sweet roll. She could eat no more than two bites before she felt nauseated. "Cole's at work for awhile," she blurted out. "He'll be back as soon as he finishes." With that she poured herself a glass of milk, hoping to calm her queasy stomach.

"I want some," Rosemary said, her voice in the pout mood.

"Then get it yourself," Pauline ordered. "Or just go without."

"Why are you being mean to us?" Charlotte asked. "We didn't leave you."

"He's not left me," Pauline shouted. "He'll be back."

But inside, she didn't feel confident at all. Would he really come back? Then the thought hit her. Had he tired of her? Had he found another woman? She'd find a way to kill him, if that were the case. Make him regret his betrayal. Yes, she'd have to kill him.

Two weeks had gone by since Amanda visited Brooke. Brooke's advice had always been well thought out. So Amanda made her list of pro's and con's about returning to Preston. The list proved very one-sided, in favor of the pro's. All the con's were minor, except the one big one. Desertion. Against that, the other con's proved to be no more than mere nit-picks.

She sat looking at the list, and feeling foolish. Not one item on the list had she needed to review. The only real consideration: could she forgive Preston? And if Jackie had spoken the truth about Pauline, causing her to go after Preston, why had he fallen for it?

Pauline should be back from Paris by now, so why not call? Just as she reached for the phone, it rang, startling her.

"Hello, Amanda. Come have dinner with us." The voice was Molly's, jovial and light. "We miss seeing you."

"But," Amanda began, not immediately thinking of an excuse not to go, so Molly cut her off quickly.

"Nonsense," Molly countered. "I need to talk to you about something important. Besides, it will do you good to get out of that apartment for awhile. I'll call Preston at the office and have him pick you up. See you about six." She hung up without giving Amanda a chance to refuse.

Resigned to eating out, Amanda hung up, but she wondered what Molly had up her sleeve.

CHAPTER 26

When Preston called Amanda, she told him she would drive to Kent early to talk to his aunts. She didn't want to ride with him. Disappointment rang in his voice, but Amanda remained firm.

At the old house, she found Molly alone.

"Hallie's out with that man again. Won't be home for supper, so we can talk without her knowing." Molly looked pained, as if she ached all over.

Puzzled, Amanda asked, "What man?"

"That George, what ever-his-name is."

Amanda couldn't help laughing. "He's a great guy, Molly. Why do you worry about it?"

"Because... she's getting silly notions. Talks about a ring...and everything."

Amanda sobered, realizing how concerned Molly had become. "She'll be fine. George is perfectly honorable. We've known him for eight years."

"At her age, I don't worry about that," Molly replied soberly.

Amanda thought for a moment. "Let's sit down and consider this. Are you afraid she'll marry him?" She didn't know much about the situation between Hallie and George, so how could she give advice? Didn't even know how long they'd been seeing each other.

"What if she does?" Molly sat on the sofa, wringing her hands. "Where does that leave me? We've always been together. Never even vacationed separately."

"But you'd only be two houses apart," Amanda tried to console her. "It's not as if she'd be moving any distance away."

As they talked, Molly's eyes filled with tears. "Just the same, she'd be gone from here." Then after a pause, she added, "It means I've got to look for a place on my own. Live alone for the rest of my life. Wish I'd made more effort to find a place when we first came. Got her out of temptation's way."

Amanda couldn't stop a smile from spreading over her face, though she'd prevented herself from laughing outright. "Do you think Hallie's in love with George?"

"Silly old thing acts like it."

"If she marries him, you needn't look for a house at all. I'd love to have you live with me." She hoped that would cheer up Molly, lighten her mood, but she doubted it would.

"Preston's already offered me a job here, same as I'm doing now. But you know, without Hallie to rib, things won't be the same."

"Let's wait and see what happens. We can make plans from there. Hallie might just be giving you a hard time. You do boss her about, you know."

"You think she's just getting even?" Molly brightened at the prospect.

Shaking her head, Amanda replied, "Doesn't sound like Hallie, does it?"

"No. That's what bothers me the most."

"Why?"

"Doesn't show much concern over leaving me. I don't think she cares about me any more."

Now Amanda did laugh. "That's crazy talk, and you know it. She still loves you. It's just that if she's deeply in love with George, the old bonds loosen and lose their luster, for awhile. Take second place, so to speak. It will right itself in time. Hallie isn't uncaring. She's probably overwhelmed with her new thrilling prospects."

Molly seemed to be mulling it over. Then she grumped, "Damned old man should have kept himself to himself, not befuddle my poor Hallie."

"She's not befuddled, Molly. And I know what I'm talking about. I'm the befuddled one." And it's something I've got to cure, she silently told herself. "Things will work out, you'll see."

At home later, she realized part of her problem came about over the feeling of isolation. She was lonely. Ever since her marriage to Preston, she'd lost contact with all her friends except Brooke.

Lifting the phone, she intended to talk to Brooke, but instead she lowered the receiver to the cradle. This problem she'd have to settle without outside help. Only she could make the necessary changes, bring about the needed moves to get her life back on track. She'd dwelt on the past too long. Time to move forward.

Preston had called Pauline several times over as many days. She never answered, so he surmised she hadn't returned from Paris. As he plopped onto the overstuffed chair in the living room, he thought about his sister. How could she spend so much time shopping for clothes? She never wore anything decent, just jeans or short skirts and flimsy blouses.

What a pain she turned out to be. He wished he'd never promised his parents he'd look after her, when what he wanted most, at the moment, was to get away for awhile, forget about her.

Now that Cole had returned from his vacation, he knew he could, but even the business worries bothered him now. They never had before. Then Hallie had confided in him that she would soon marry George. Molly hadn't been told, which bothered him a great deal.

As for Amanda, she seemed no closer to taking him back than she had when he first returned. She'd moved out of the house, and refused to ride home with him the other night. He knew his wooing efforts were going nowhere.

He needed to do something to get his mind off the whole lot. Like the time he spent with Brooke's children. He'd really enjoyed that weekend, enjoyed giving the piggyback rides down the hall. And Candy proved to be an absolute charmer. What a stroke of luck for Brooke to be able to get those wonderful girls, he thought. A surge of envy filled him. Yes, he'd like to see them all again.

Milo and Jackie had met with their respective attorneys. Though Milo felt a strong undercurrent of hate from Jackie, still, she'd agreed to his conditions for the divorce settlement. And he'd seen the fire of hatred in her eyes when Agatha had accompanied him to the office, though she waited outside in the reception room.

He watched Jackie sign the legal papers, her face turned away from him. The face he'd once adored, cherished even. Why had the marriage turned sour, so bitter? He'd made every effort to be a good husband. Tried to keep her happy and contented. Given her everything she wanted.

After she finished signing the papers, she looked up at him for a moment, with a far-away look in her eyes, then lowered them. Yes, he thought, her eyes were never content with the present, always looking for something or someone else.

Well, now he'd soon be free of them, and Agatha had no such look about her. Good old Agatha, she's one in a million that woman.

With Jackie out of the house, Amanda visited her father more often. They'd actually become friends. He appreciated her silence about Jackie and Preston, though he knew she must still be hurting over it. For him the hurt had vanished weeks ago.

When he and Jackie left the attorney's office, neither spoke, nor did Jackie look at the waiting Agatha. He took her arm and together they left the building, each smiling broadly.

A week after Cole disappeared from Pauline's car, she became impatient for his return. Several times she'd gone downstairs to call his office. But each time she couldn't bring herself to do it. She'd give him more time, perhaps another week. He should be back by then. What a wonderful reunion they'd have. She'd call him next week and tell him to bring ice cream with him. They'd all enjoy that treat.

All her friends were angry with her, angry enough to refuse to eat. Pauline ate some, but just a bite or two filled her. When she spoke to Rosemary, Rosemary refused to answer, turning her head away. All the rest were the same. "Go ahead and sulk," she ordered, "See if I care."

Twilla began to sing softly to herself. "Let me hear you," Pauline encouraged. "You have such a beautiful voice." The voice was a low and gravelly alto, but anything to break the stagnant silence pleased Pauline.

She couldn't place the song Twilla sang, though she'd heard it before. Asking about it wouldn't bring the answer, so she concentrated on the tune, trying to add the words in her mind. The words, "some still day" came to mind, though nothing more.

"Sing it louder," Pauline demanded.

But Twilla continued singing softly.

Pauline got up off the wrinkled blankets and hobbled to the small, dirty window. She pushed aside the curtains and looked out just in time to see a man get out of a car in her driveway. He headed for her front door.

Frightened, she dropped the curtains, and said, "Shut up, Twilla. Someone's coming to the door. Now be quiet, or we'll all be taken away." She dropped to her bed in panic, and pulled up the covers to hide.

After several minutes, she heard movement below, then footsteps on the stairs. She held her breath, straining to hear every movement. Her heart pounded loudly enough for everyone to hear, but she couldn't quiet it.

Someone called out, "Pauline, are you home?"

She couldn't place the familiar voice, nor had she recognized the man or his car. How did he get into the house? Did he have a key? She wanted to shout to him, tell him to get out of her house, but that would expose her hiding place. Jeopardize all of them.

Now she wished Cole were here to help her and her friends. He'd know exactly what to do. Yes, she couldn't wait any longer for him to come home. Tomorrow, she'd call him and let him do the worrying.

CHAPTER 27

Hallie wasn't home when Preston arrived. He wouldn't ask Molly about it for fear of starting another tirade. She never knew when to end it. He felt compassion for them both, but there didn't seem to be a way he could help. Molly, tight-lipped, finally said, "She's out with that man again." Perspiration dampened the graying bangs on her forehead, parting them in the middle. She brushed them to one side. "Where will it ever end?" she muttered, sounding as if she might cry any moment.

Preston put an arm over her shoulders as she hurried to pass, then guided her to a chair at the kitchen table. "Molly," he began, "you worry too much. If Hallie marries George, just think of her happiness. It will probably be the best thing ever to happen to her. You don't begrudge her that, do you?"

Molly sniffled, and averted her eyes. "But she's acting so silly," she protested.

Preston remembered those early days with Amanda. He, too, had acted silly, made statements, which on the surface, didn't make much sense. He smiled. "It's all part of the love sickness, Molly. Surely you can forgive her that? If you'd ever been in love, you'd know."

Her head snapped around, her chin rose. "Who says I haven't been in love?" she demanded.

If she had, Preston knew nothing of it. "Then remember back to how you felt."

"No way!" she countered.

"Why is that?" he asked, puzzled by her curt, abrupt response.

She looked directly at him before lowering her head. Then in a muted voice she said, "He never told me he was married. I had to find it out myself, the hard way. Took me for a fool, he did. Broke my heart, too. That's the kind of thing Hallie has in store for her."

Preston cringed, then said, "I'm sorry about that, Molly, but George isn't married, nor is he a cheat." He paused. "I never knew about your love."

"Didn't want anyone to know what a fool I made of myself. Didn't even tell Hallie."

"If it's any help, I understand your feelings. I'm going though the same thing now. Amanda no longer loves me, of that I'm sure. It's all my fault, of course, but one has to get on with life, as you well know."

As they talked, the front door opened and closed, then Hallie burst into the kitchen.

Molly gasped, and Preston couldn't help but stare.

"You silly old fool!" Molly shouted. "What have you done to yourself?"

A smiling Hallie stood just inside the doorway. Her hair had been dyed light brown, and short curls lay against her head. She'd had her first permanent. To Preston, she looked wonderful, almost beautiful.

"You look great." He stood up to hug her.

"No she doesn't," Molly countered. "She looks like...like...like a..." She didn't finish, but rushed past Hallie though the door way and out of the room. They could hear her rush up the stairs.

Silently, Hallie walked to the window and stood looking out. Finally, she turned to face Preston. "Seems she can't accept any changes."

"She'll get over it," Preston insisted, hoping he spoke the truth.

"Not her," Hallie said. "She has to be in charge." She dropped her purse on the table, turned and looked out the window again. "Thinks her attitude is going to stop me, but it's not. Done most everything she wanted all my life. Not now." She turned to face Preston. "Do you think I'm wrong?"

He looked at the transformation of Hallie. What a pity both women hadn't taken the time to care about their looks before now. "No, you're not wrong. I love you both, as you well know, but Molly will have to accept whatever you do. I'll support you, Hallie, in any way I can."

Hallie smiled as if a load had been lifted from her shoulders. She stretched out her left hand. "Want to see my ring? I think I like jewelry, now that I'm wearing some. Think I'll buy a necklace to go with this."

"It's beautiful, Hallie," he said, as he took her hand to look closely at the solitaire.

She laughed, her hazel eyes twinkling with pleasure. "From George," she said as she blushed. "I'm finally going to be a bride. Can you believe that?"

Jackie paced the floor of her apartment. Its drab furnishings depressed her. Olive green furniture on brown carpeting set her nerves ajar, even on this sunlit morning. She shook her head. I'll soon be out of here, living in Paris. Free to do just as I please. Her mood improved at the thought.

She stopped to look out the window. All she could see were the brick sides of other buildings. Hunting for an apartment on such short notice had proved difficult. She had to take what she could get, though the location had been handy to some of her favorite shops. She seldom needed to use her car. She'd sell it. Wouldn't have a car in Paris, or she'd be driving crazy like Pauline in all that frightful traffic.

The sight of Pauline rushing around the parking lot, looking for the mannequin, came to mind. What did she want with a fiberglass dummy? Did Preston know just how far from reality Pauline's mind had slipped?

She must be terribly out of touch, dragging a mannequin around town with her. A real fruitcake. Why hadn't Preston done something about her? Taken her to a doctor, or something.

She began to smile as a new idea took wing. Perhaps Preston wasn't with Amanda again. Neither confirmed it when she saw them weeks before. "It's worth a try," she murmured, feeling renewed self-confidence. She could call Preston under the pretense of telling him about Pauline. In truth, she felt she should make the call anyway, a parting kindness, even if it didn't lead to something more pleasurable.

She poured herself a glass of red wine to build her courage, then stood before a mirror. She raised the glass to salute what might have been, or might yet still be. "To you, Preston," she began, "and the joys of forbidden love." She drank, then she lifted the receiver to do her kind deed.

The call from Jackie angered Preston. He didn't want to answer it, but couldn't tell his secretary to lie for him. "Put her on," he said through clenched teeth.

"Yes, Jackie, what is it." He knew he sounded unfriendly, he could feel it in his tightened throat, but that's how things were.

After a moment's pause, she answered, "It's about Pauline."

"What about her? She's in Paris."

"No she's not."

"I went to see her yesterday and she wasn't home," he countered.

"I saw her yesterday shopping for groceries, right here in town, and she's crazy, Preston. You'd better do something about her driving in such a state. She's going to kill someone, or herself."

"What?" Had he heard her right?

"Like I said. She's acting crazy. Talking to a male dummy like it was a person." She went on to tell him just what she had witnessed. "Do something for her, the poor thing."

Preston, convinced of what he'd just heard, said, "Thanks, Jackie. I'll get right to it." He hung up, confused as to how to start.

He hurried to Cole's office, to tell him about it, and ask for advice, but Cole was on the phone, saying, "What are you talking about?" As Preston listened, Cole scribbled the word, "Pauline" on a note pad. Cole then put his hand over the receiver and whispered, "Get on the line, quickly."

Rushing back to his office, Preston gently picked up Cole's line, not knowing what to expect.

Pauline sounded harsh and bitter as she said, "That's right. You can't leave me. I want you back here today. Do you hear me?"

Preston gasped as Cole quietly replied, "Where is back here, Pauline?"

"With me and my friends, here at my house. You know where."

Sounding incredulous, Cole said, "Why do you think I was ever there with you?"

Pauline began to scream. "You've been with me for weeks. Slept with me. You can't desert me now. All the girls think you've left me." She calmed down before she spoke again. "We all need you, Cole. Some man got into the house yesterday, called out to me, but I didn't answer. Please come back today."

As if stalling for time, Cole asked, "Why didn't you answer the intruder?"

"Because he wanted to take us away from here. We need you here to look after us. Protect us."

"But Pauline, I've not been to your house for years." Annoyance began to sound in his voice.

"Don't do this to me." she shouted, "Or I'll make you pay for it."

Preston couldn't listen any longer. He returned the receiver to the cradle, leaned back in the chair, too shocked and worried to fully comprehend. How could Pauline think such things? Cole would never have been with her.

His door swung open and Cole rushed in. His heavy eyebrows knit together over equally dark eyes. "How much did you hear?"

"Enough to worry me."

"Well, do something." With a deep sigh, Cole plopped onto a chair opposite Preston. "I'm worried. The whole thing is a lie. I've never been near her place, Preston, let alone slept with her. She's gone over the edge." His face grew pale as he spoke.

Preston nodded. "Jackie had just called to say she'd seen Pauline acting like a fool at the grocery store. I'm not sure how to handle this."

"Get her to a doctor. Now! She's just crazy enough to make good her threat to come after me."

"She wouldn't do that," Preston replied, shaking his head without conviction.

"I'm not ready to take that chance."

Preston dreaded what had to be done, but reason dictated he act fast. Try to get her into some medical facility. "I'll call Amanda and see if she'll help me."

"Why subject her to that? You've done her enough damage as it is. Besides, Pauline hates her, and isn't to be trusted. She could well attack Amanda." Cole unbuttoned his black suit jacket and unloosened his maroon tie as he talked. "If it were me, I'd take along a police officer, just in case you need help."

Preston shook his head. "I don't want to frighten her. A policeman would scare her to death."

Cole pursed his lips for a moment, then said, "That's not possible. Not in my book."

"But..." He didn't finish. "How do I tell Pauline what has to be done?"

"Don't waste your time explaining. She won't understand anyway. You'd better start by calling her doctor. Get him to commit her to some institution, before she gets violent."

After some thought, Preston said, "You're right." Reluctantly he lifted the phone and punched out the doctor's number. "Let's hope it can be done today," he said, more as a prayer than a certainty.

Amanda had just arrived home as the phone began to ring. She dropped her bag of groceries to the table, then picked up the phone. "Hello?"

"I hate you, you're vile, mean, deceitful. You've ruined everything. You made him go," A tearful Pauline choked out. "It's all because of you."

Amanda, amazed at the sound of Pauline's voice, as well as the accusations, said, "What are you talking about?"

"You know. Everyone knows what you did."

"What did I do?"

"Killed it, that's what." She sounded angry now, and bitter. "You'll pay for it." She coughed several times as if to clear her throat. "We'll all see that you pay."

"We?"

"My friends and me."

Amanda immediately assumed Pauline meant the mannequins, though the threat was ridiculous. "What's wrong, Pauline. Can I help you?"

"I have witnesses. We'll all testify."

"About what?" Amanda said, not making any sense of Pauline's ranting.

"All about what you did."

"You're talking crazy, Pauline." The moment she said it, she wished she hadn't. She hastily said, "Tell me what's wrong."

"I'm not crazy," Pauline shouted. "Rosemary knows all about you, too."

"Have you talked to Preston?"

Pauline laughed. "He's not my friend."

"He cares about you, Pauline," Amanda said, trying hard to handle the situation tactfully.

Pauline began to cry. "Only Cole cared about me. Now you've killed that."

"It's not true," Amanda said. "Are you at home, Pauline?"

"Yes."

"I'll come over to help you."

Pauline sniffled. "I hate strangers in my house, especially men. They come all the time to see me, but I won't let them in. One sneaked in yesterday, pretended to know me. Called to me several times. I didn't answer." She laughed now, a high-pitched laugh, a cackle. "If I know they're coming, I leave," she bragged.

"How would you know they're coming?" She couldn't believe Pauline had men pestering her.

"They call all the time. They're in love with me, but I only care about Cole." She paused. "But you killed that."

"When you leave, where do you go?"

"I won't tell you, or anyone. It's my secret."

"Can I help you?" Amanda, filled with anger at Preston for letting Pauline get to this state, felt compelled to help.

"I don't want your help. Don't you dare come near me, or you'll pay for it."

Confused now, Amanda said, "Then why did you call me?"

"I didn't call you. I never call you." With that she slammed down the receiver, leaving Amanda more worried than ever.

CHAPTER 28

Amanda immediately called Preston's office, only to learn he had gone to see Pauline. Cole told her about the call from Pauline. Anxious to be of help, Amanda slipped into her coat and drove to the old house. Preston was parked in the driveway with his car door open as she drove up. He looked puzzled.

"Pauline called me," she told him, as they each got out of their cars.

"She called Cole, too." he replied, as he buttoned his jacket against the cold.

"What are you going to do?" Amanda put on her gloves as they walked toward the house. The chilly late November weather was biting, and the strong winds off the ocean compounded the problem.

"Get her to the doctor. He'll take care of the rest, thank goodness." He seemed anxious to be relieved of the responsibility.

They hurried up the steps of the porch, Preston with his key in hand. "Jackie also called to tell me Pauline has been hauling a mannequin around town with her. Even talking to it."

The mention of Jackie's name brought no response from Amanda. Not a flinch, nor a hint of anger, as they entered the dark, musty-smelling hallway. Two envelopes lay on the floor beneath the mail slot. Preston put them on the hallstand. "Pauline, it's me," he called out. "Where are you? We need to talk." He paused for a moment to listen, but no response came.

They searched the kitchen first, but found nothing out of the ordinary, just the usual messy cabinet. Pauline didn't believe in cleaning up, unless everything had been used first. Then they searched every room on the main floor without any success.

"She told me she leaves if anyone comes," Amanda said. "She wouldn't say where she goes."

"Did she threaten you?"

Amanda nodded. "With the mannequins' revenge, poor thing." She couldn't help smiling.

"It's hard to believe she's this bad," he replied, as he led the way up the creaking stairs. He glanced quickly at the ceiling, where the old attic entrance used to be. The repair to close it up had been expertly done, and was not visible.

"The mannequins are gone," Amanda gasped, as she looked into Pauline's bedroom. "All of them."

"How many?"

"Six in all."

"Jackie said Pauline had one in the car, but it was evidently stolen while she shopped."

Amanda faced him. "Which one, do you know?"

"According to Jackie, a male dummy."

"She must have bought a new one. She had no male before." Amanda couldn't understand why Pauline would buy another, though Pauline had inherited enough money to spend it however she liked.

"What does she want with those things, anyway?"

Surprised at the question, Amanda replied, "They are her friends. Didn't you know?"

He shook his head, but didn't answer.

"Well, you should have known," she snapped. "Pauline had no friends. You certainly knew that." He looked confused, as if he didn't understand. "How come you didn't?"

He stared at her. "She never told me."

Exasperated, Amanda said, "Told you? Do you have to be told everything? Can't you do a little thinking for yourself? I've been telling you about her problems for some time. You never listened."

"I'm sorry," he replied. "I didn't fully realize."

"You never do."

They walked through the rest of the rooms, but didn't find Pauline. Yet Amanda felt a strange coldness seep through her, as if the house had gone unheated for some time. A penetrating cold sent shivers over her as she followed Preston down the stairs.

Again at the front door, he said, with a hint of disgust, "She's playing games with me again."

"Again?"

Taking a deep breath, he said, "Always, as a kid, she set me up for one thing or another. Always trying to make me look foolish, a phone call to be answered that never came, a friend at the door who wasn't there. Her favorite game, until I moved out."

Amanda scoffed, "She also set you up with Jackie. Why didn't you realize that? What makes you so blind, where she's concerned?"

Preston opened the front door, then turned to face her. "Dread. Pure and simple dread." Without a blink, he continued. "I promised Mother I'd never institutionalize Pauline, never send her to a 'nut house' again, as Mother called it."

Angered and disappointed at his insensitivity to Pauline's needs, she said, "How foolish of your mother to force such a promise from you, and just as foolish for you to have kept it. Turning your head doesn't make the problem disappear, nor diminish your responsibility in all this."

"I don't need a lecture from you," he said. "Not from you." He went out the door, locking it after Amanda.

"We can't let it go on like this, Preston," she protested, pulling at his jacket sleeve to turn him around. "She needs help. Now!"

He faced her. "I know. I'll wait around until she comes home, and take it from there."

"Do you want me to wait with you?"

He hesitated a moment. "No, you go home. I'll call you if I need you. I'll sit here and wait it out."

Relieved, she said good-bye. As she drove away, she saw him get into his car, frowning as if he awaited some unspoken doom.

"The man is waiting in the car," Pauline told her friends, as she stood before the small window. She'd pulled open the curtains only an inch or two. She laughed. "He thinks I'll be coming home soon. We'll all have to be quiet."

"You have to be quiet," Twilla objected. "You're the only one moving about."

Pauline glowered at her. "I'll take a stick to you, if you don't hold your tongue. A thin stick lay on the floor beside the stairway opening. In the summer, she used it to prop open the window.

Twilla laughed. "You can't even lift it any longer, let alone swing it." She wore Pauline's favorite leather skirt and jacket, which angered Pauline. They'd fought over it earlier. Twilla prevailed.

"One of these days, I'll show you. And I'll make you take off my best clothes." Too weak to do anything about it now, Pauline struggled back to her bed.

She looked at the bags of food on the floor, lying just where she'd dropped them. A loaf of bread had been opened some time before, and partly eaten by mice. The package of butter horns had one missing. She'd taken a bite of one sweet roll, but couldn't eat it. The mice had nibbled away at it, leaving only the center, and finished off some of the rest. Food now made her nauseous. What little water she drank seemed too much for her stomach to hold, causing it to cramp.

She'd tried many times to get her friends to eat, but like herself, all claimed not to be hungry.

Rosemary, her dearest friend, stood hunched over, as if in pain.

"All of you had better have something to eat," Pauline cautioned. "You need to keep up your strength."

"We can't eat."

"Come lie down with me then, Rosemary."

"I'm too weak. I can't move alone."

Pauline's own physical condition had deteriorated rapidly. She struggled to her feet, then shuffled across the wooden floor to Rosemary. Taking her by the waist, she guided her back to the bed. Immediately, Rosemary flopped to the blanket and groaned.

Seriously worried for her friends, Pauline said, "All of you had better try to eat."

"We can't," they replied in unison.

"Please try," Pauline begged. "For my sake."

With a shake of her head, Rosemary said. "I just want to be with you."

Puzzled, Pauline replied, "You are with me."

"I mean always."

"I don't understand," Pauline said. "Move over and I'll lie down with you." As they settled on the small bed, Pauline soon drifted off to sleep, while Rosemary lay wide-eyed, staring at the ceiling.

Preston sat in the car for three hours, occasionally running the car motor to warm it. His feet continued to hurt from the cold, and he grew stiff. He got out of the car to walk on the driveway and limber up. He stamped his feet lightly as he walked.

He couldn't understand where Pauline might be for such a long time. He called Cole on his cell phone, half expecting Pauline had made another call. She hadn't, so he then called Amanda. She didn't answer. He continued to stamp his feet and mumble to himself. Where in the world had Pauline gone? Had she driven?

Curious, he went to the garage beside the house. He found the car inside. He looked at it for some minutes. Finally he went to feel the car hood. Stone cold. The old Chevy hadn't been driven today.

After closing the garage door, he turned to look into the back yard. Weeds grew thick, as if no one had been in the yard for years. The garden had been his mother's pride. How could Pauline let it deteriorate into this tangle of weeds?

Unnerved, he sat on the steps at the back door. As children, he and Pauline, under pressure, had often helped pull weeds and water the flowerbeds. No longer were the beds visible. The only familiar plant lay draped across the back fence. A dark red rose in need of trimming.

Often, while watering the garden, he would dream of how wonderful it would be to get away from Pauline and her crazy antics. Well, he'd been away now for twenty years, and still she haunted his life like a black shadow. And he'd made a mess of his own life as well. Something only a dumb ass would do.

As he sat, he wondered if he could have done anything to help Pauline earlier? Once he had tried, just after he moved away, but it turned out all wrong. Even his parents resented his efforts to get Pauline to see a specialist. She'd been institutionalized once without any improvement. He'd thought another doctor might be more helpful. He gave up after a terrible argument with his parents.

The pungent odor of dead weeds, molding leaves and damp earth drove him from the yard and back inside his car.

Could Pauline actually be in the house? Hiding in some closet. They'd never checked closets, but why would she hide in closets?

Before he turned the car key, he looked at the attic window. The old lace curtain must have hung there ever since his father boarded up the attic entrance some years before. As a child, Pauline used to get up into the attic and hide, so their parents boarded it up and painted it over.

Had he checked on it closely enough? Could Pauline have reopened it without him noticing? On a hunch, Preston went into the house again, and climbed the stairs to look at where the old attic entrance had been. No way he thought, as he stared at it. Satisfied, he checked all the closets and found nothing, so went back to his car. No point in waiting around any longer. He'd try again tomorrow. Right now he needed a hot shower.

CHAPTER 29

Hallie arrived home in the early evening, just after Preston and Molly had eaten. She came down the hall with hesitant steps, causing Preston some anxiety.

When she appeared in the doorway, he asked, "Is everything all right?" Her flushed face gave no hint of what bothered her.

"I'm just fine," she replied, looking tense.

"You certainly don't look it," Molly said.

"Nevertheless I am. In fact, I'm walking on air. Want to know why?" She watched Molly closely, with squinting eyes.

"Not really," Molly said. She stared at her sister with unblinking eyes, then looked away.

"I'll tell you anyway. Since you've been dead set against my engagement to George, I wanted to end the constant tirades. Since two o'clock today, I've been Mrs. George Beston." She braced herself against the doorframe, as if awaiting the next tirade.

"You damned old fool," Molly cried out. "Never could trust you out of my sight."

Without a flinch, Hallie replied, "Since you can't be civil about this, I'll be out of your sight from now on. Thank the Lord. If you change your ways, call me. Otherwise this is good-bye."

Ignoring Molly, Preston went to her, kissing her cheek as he hugged her. "I wish you a world of happiness, Hallie."

Molly sat stiff-necked and pale. She did not look at her sister. Preston felt great pity as he watched her cup her chin with her hand, palm over her mouth, thumb and index finger rubbing her cheeks, as if to stop from crying. She then eyed her twin up and down. "Well, now that you've gone and done the damned fool thing, why are you back here?" Her voice quivered as she spoke.

"To get some of my things." Hallie said. "George will be back for me in a half hour. To save you from seeing him, I'll meet him outside." She turned and walked away.

Exasperated, Preston said, "Molly! You might have wished her well. She deserves that much from you."

Tight-lipped and teary eyed, Molly pushed away from the table and left the room.

In a state of unease, Preston cleared off the dishes and put them in the dishwasher. He couldn't reason out how to help Molly and Hallie over the turn of events. Nor could he stop his mind from jumping back to his sister. "Misery comes in sets of three," he could hear his mother say.

He hadn't told Molly what had happened earlier, that Pauline needed medical attention at once. Even if he couldn't get her into an institution, surely some sort of medication would help. She certainly shouldn't live alone any longer, but where then?

In his home? The thought of her in the same house with him sent bone-chilling shivers down his spine, but where else could she go? He felt a deep conviction that in the end, he'd have to house her.

Pauline awoke and turned to face Rosemary, who still stared at the ceiling. "Wake up," Pauline said, but no response was forthcoming.

"Rosemary! Rosemary!" she called out, as she struggled to sit up.

"She's dead, you see," Twilla said. "We're all dead, you see. We're all dead, you see," she chanted, in cold-blooded tones. The others soon joined in the chant.

"Shut up," Pauline replied. She managed to get to her feet, then pull Rosemary across the bed, where she soon rolled onto the floor and lay still. "Get up. Here, I'll help you." The others kept up the rhythmic chant, in a sing-song fashion.

When Rosemary still didn't move, Pauline tried to lift her, but failed. "Come help me," she called to the others. "We need your help." She grunted as she struggled to get Rosemary on her feet, while the chant continued.

Finally, she turned to the others, but they all looked away, ignoring her completely, while they continued their droning words. "If Rosemary dies, so do the rest of you. I won't keep you without her," Pauline shouted.

She crossed the floor with unsteady, shuffling steps, intending to make the others help her. She grabbed Twilla's arm to pull her, but instead of walking, Twilla fell face down onto the floor, and lay as still as Rosemary. The chanting grew louder, though Twilla's voice was stilled.

Tears came to Pauline's eyes. "Why won't you help me?" she asked. Without waiting for a reply, she again said, "Please help me."

No one moved. "You're not my friends any longer," she told them. "None of you."

Totally unsteady on her feet, she lost her balance and fell against Clodette, knocking her over. Grabbing for anything to steady herself, she brought down the next mannequin. Only two remained standing. She looked up at them. "Please help me up."

As she watched them, her vision blurred, and they seemed to be swaying and shaking their heads. They continued the chanting.

Her breathing became shallow and in gasps. As she struggled to get up, neither of the mannequins moved to help her. She turned to her stomach, and pressing her hands on the floor, she managed to get to her knees. Panting, she didn't move for several minutes.

With new resolve, she crawled along the floor on her hands and knees. She reached Rosemary, then stretched over her to reach the covers from the bed. With great effort, she pulled them over Rosemary and herself. "I'll keep you warm," she whispered into Rosemary's ear. She shivered so hard her whole body shook, inside and out.

As she lay, her breathing became very shallow, her eyes closed. From the back of her mind came the vision of herself as a child, lying in bed. A beautiful woman sat on the side of the bed, singing softly and caressing

Pauline's face. When she stopped singing, she began the nightly prayer ritual.

Pauline remembered it well and in a whisper joined in saying the words. "Now...I...lay...me...down...to sleep." Her breathing slowed, her words trailed off, and the chanting ceased.

Amanda awoke to an early morning phone call.

"I'm paying off Jackie today," Milo said, his voice light and bright. "What do you think of that?"

"Wonderful."

"She's off to Paris at the end of the week. Good riddance, I say."

Amanda felt no concern for Jackie's activities, though her deep dislike of Jackie remained unchanged.

"So, we're having a celebration Sunday, a big party. You'll be here, won't you?"

"Wouldn't miss it," Amanda said.

"What about Preston?"

"What about him?" She didn't understand why the question.

"Have the two of you made up. Got back together?"

"No."

"Good. I wouldn't want him here."

"You needn't worry, he wouldn't come under any circumstances."

Milo grumped, "You'd think I was at fault."

Amanda smiled. "Maybe we both were, a little."

"I don't buy that. Not for one moment." His angry voice came through so loud, Amanda had to remove the receiver from her ear.

"Watch that blood-pressure," she cautioned. "So, how is Agatha these days?"

His voice changed. "Preparing her trousseau. We'll be married just as soon as that divorce decree is in my hands."

"Well, good for you."

"Best move I ever made." He paused. "Since your mother died, I mean." He sounded apologetic.

"We all make mistakes," she said. "Sometimes we just don't see them, until it's too late. Tell Agatha hello for me."

She had no sooner hung up the phone than it rang again.

"What the heck are you up to?" a jovial Brooke demanded. "You're neglecting your responsibilities around here. No visits to your nieces, no phone calls, no letters. We won't willingly stand for that."

Amanda laughed. "Things here should ease off in a few days."

"Well, when you come, the girls insist you bring their Uncle Preston, too. They love him."

"That ought to please him." Amanda said.

"But don't bring any toys this time. They have too many as it is, though they don't think so."

"Nothing? I can't bring anything at all?"

"Don't sound so abused. They all like gumdrops. You can bring some of them, if you have to bring anything."

"Yes, ma'am," Amanda replied, pretending to be rebuffed. "Whatever you say."

Before going to work, Preston stopped by Pauline's house, hoping to find her home. He let himself in, but couldn't find her, and got no response no matter how loudly he called out to her.

At work, he found it impossible to concentrate. Every hour he called his sister, but she never answered. He paced as Cole came in to see him.

"She's playing hide-and-seek with you," Cole said. "You'll have to locate her soon."

"Where do I look? Seattle is a big place to start hunting." His frustration nagged like a toothache.

"She's never lived anywhere but in your parent's home. Why would you look somewhere else?"

"But she's not there," Preston objected. "I've searched the place a couple of times."

With a frown, Cole said, "Any basement? Attic?"

"No basement. The old attic is boarded up." He went on to explain why.

"Garage?" Cole asked.

With a shrug of resignation, Preston replied, "I've looked there, too."

"Look again. I don't like the fact that she's out there free. Makes me nervous. She's crazy enough to do anything."

The phone rang, interrupting the conversation.

"Preston," Amanda said, "Let's canvas Pauline's neighborhood, ask if anyone has seen Pauline of late."

He didn't know why he hadn't thought of it himself. "Good idea."

"I'll meet you there. What time can you make it?"

"In an hour," he said. "Bring an umbrella." It had poured all morning. When he hung up, he said to Cole, "We're going to ask her neighbors if they've seen her."

"I'd go help, if Amos weren't coming in with his list of purchases in Hong-Kong." Amos was their best buyer.

"I know," Preston replied. "Thanks for the offer anyway."

The clock hands moved slowly the next half-hour. Every time Preston looked, the minute hand had barely changed. Finally, he took the clock off the wall, thinking the battery needed replacing, though he didn't have a replacement at the moment. He remained standing, then shoved the papers on his desk to one side.

Too disconcerted to work, he left the office and drove to Amanda's apartment, intending to take her to his sister's house. By now, his mood matched the weather, dark and brooding.

He climbed the stairs and rapped on the door.

Amanda answered it. "Hey, you're early. What's up?" She stood back to let him enter.

"I simply couldn't sit still any longer. I'm getting frantic about Pauline." He walked in and dropped his raincoat and hat to the sofa. "I can't do anything for her until we find her. It's driving me nuts."

She looked at him critically, scowling as she watched him. "Shall we go over right now?"

He took a deep breath. "I could use a cup of coffee, first, if that's OK."

"Sure. Come into the kitchen."

He followed. As he sat at the kitchen table, he said, "I think this is an emergency. I feel it in my bones." He shivered because he felt so useless, so inept.

"Are you cold?" she asked.

"Not really, but my whole insides seem to be shaking. What if Pauline is lying somewhere out there in the cold. She could easily die out there, alone." After a deep breath, he added, "I was wishing I could turn the past around."

Amanda set the coffee on the table, then sat down.

"Perhaps we should call the police," she suggested.

"They'll only tell us she hasn't been missing long enough for them to get involved.

They bolted down their coffee in silence, then started out for Pauline's.

CHAPTER 30

On the way to Pauline's, Amanda told Preston about the calls from Milo and Brooke. His scowl softened into a smile, when she told him the girls called him "Uncle."

"The only bright spots in my life these past few months," he said, glancing at her out of the corner of his eye. "They're wonderful kids."

"Yes, they are."

He paused before speaking again. "Let's go down to see them, when this business with Pauline is settled."

Amanda nodded and smiled to herself. He obviously took her willingness to go with him for granted.

"I may have to bring Pauline to my place, if all else fails," he began to explain, a touch of irony in his voice. "Never thought it would come to this."

She stared at him, knowing what such a move would entail. "Molly won't stay, you know," she cautioned.

He nodded. "I realize that. I'll have to make arrangements for a nurse or a companion for Pauline. I'll work that out. She'll need supervision full time, I'm afraid."

She started to speak, but stopped herself. Never had she imagined he would ever consider taking in Pauline. What a bitter pill to swallow.

Preston parked in front of the garage, then checked to see if the car was inside. It was. They went into the house, he calling out to his sister. The unheated house creaked as they walked. No answer came to Preston's call, so they began the search. They'd check with the neighbors afterward.

Every kitchen closet and cabinet was opened. The cupboards held little food, mostly canned beets and beans. "Good heavens! Is this all she eats. I don't understand her or where she could be," Preston said. "It doesn't look as if she's cooked in a month of Sundays."

When Amanda opened the refrigerator, green mold covered the corners and edges of the white enamel. She quickly closed the door, pulling back in disgust. She turned the kitchen light switch. Nothing happened. "She couldn't cook without electricity. That's why the house is so cold, and the refrigerator moldy."

"Why would the electric be turned off?"

"She probably hasn't paid the bill. You should check into it." More puzzled than ever, she climbed the stairs with Preston, holding on to the railing. The stairs were quite dark.

"And where are the mannequins? They should be somewhere around, but I haven't seen them." She walked first into Pauline's room, scanning it carefully, while Preston looked in other rooms. A small non-working clock sat on the bedside stand in the shadows of the heavily curtained window. She pushed back the curtains for more light.

Just how long had it been since the clock last ran? An eerie feeling crept over her. The dead silence caused her to catch her breath. She pulled the raincoat closer around her and tied the belt tightly. Still, she felt cold.

Something about the room bothered her. Where were those mannequins? When she opened the walk-in closet, she could barely see inside. As her eyes adjusted, she found Pauline's fancy new clothes were missing. Only a few old ones hung from hangers, all of them pushed to one side. How strange, she thought. Has Pauline taken her good clothes and gone back to New York or Paris?

Looking up, with what little light came from the window, she noticed an unusual pattern on the ceiling. Wooden slates marked off the area in large, oblong strips. Acoustical tiles were fitted in between. The one tile in the center didn't quite fit. It seemed to be thicker, hung lower than the rest. Perhaps it had come loose in this damp place.

Shrugging, she left the room to search another. Not locating Pauline, she and Preston left the house to canvas the neighborhood. No one had seen Pauline in days, some said weeks. All referred to her as the hermit. Pauline had never been friendly with any of them, hence, they never took much notice of her. Dejected, they returned to the car.

"Come home with me," Preston said, as they were pulling out of the driveway. "Help me get through to Molly, smooth out her resentment toward Hallie." He looked at her with a pleading smile. She nodded. He then told her what had happened between his aunts.

"What a shame, and so unnecessary."

The cold dampness of Pauline's house seemed to have sunk into Amanda's bones. The prospect of a warm fire sent little shivers of pleasure through her. She missed not having a fireplace in the apartment.

Preston said, "Maybe you can help reason with Molly. We don't need this problem just now, not with Pauline missing." he said.

"You're right," she replied, but her mind remained on Pauline. The statement about leaving the house if anyone came pricked in Amanda's mind, and she reminded Preston of it. "How would Pauline know when someone is coming to see her? She couldn't! So where is she?"

"Many things are troubling me," Preston agreed. Let's get this other business of Molly over with, then we'll concentrate on her whereabouts again, while we warm up. Mother always said, 'Troubles come in threes.' I guess she was right."

When they walked into the house, Molly was busy in the kitchen, and singing to herself. They stared at each other.

"I don't believe it," he whispered to Amanda. He helped her remove her coat, then hung both in the closet.

"That sounds good to me, Molly," Amanda called out.

Molly rushed into the hall. "Well, it's about time you showed up here." She grabbed Amanda in a bear hug. "I'm starting dinner. I hadn't expected either of you for lunch, but I'll make us each a sandwich." She turned to go back to the kitchen. "We're having guests tonight," she said over her shoulder."

"This is the last thing I want tonight, Molly. Who is it?"

"Hallie and George, that's who." She began humming as she went about her business. "It has to be done sometime, so why not now?"

Preston stared at Amanda, who stood smiling at him. "They've worked it out," he guessed out loud.

Molly turned to face him. "In a way," she replied. "Hallie came over this morning. I wasn't any too civil, until she uttered an ultimatum."

"Which was?" Preston held his breath. He didn't need any more bad news.

"She said if I force it, a choice between George and me, she'll choose him. How can I live with that? I won't let it happen, even if I have to eat crow. She's my sister, my other half." Molly blinked hard, as if forcing back tears. "So...I'll eat crow...even if I don't like the taste of it, but let's not plan on turkey for Thanksgiving. Perhaps ham or beef, but no fowl." She forced a laugh, and returned to the kitchen.

While she and Amanda prepared sandwiches for lunch, Preston built a fire in the fireplace. The three sat before the blaze to eat the sandwiches and drink coffee. Then Preston told Molly, "Pauline is missing, and her place looks and feels like a morgue. The mannequins are gone, and the place has become a dump. No electricity either."

"She'll never be right in the head," Molly said, "no matter what you try to do."

"I know. It's been a totally wasted life for her. Perhaps some day scientists will find a cure." Preston finished his sandwich and picked up the hot coffee.

"Don't hold your breath," Molly replied. "That's not where the money goes."

"When did you first know Pauline had mental problems?" Amanda asked.

"She was very small. Mother once said she noticed something different about her by the time she started to walk. She stared a great deal, as if she couldn't quite make out what she looked at. She also laughed at odd times, whenever I was hurt, or Mother and Dad had an argument."

"How strange," Amanda said.

"What was that business about the attic," Molly asked. "Your father once told me he had to board it up."

Preston remembered it well. "That's right. Pauline would disappear, on purpose, to upset the folks. She'd pull down the attic steps and hide up there, pulling them up after her. Dad had the pull-down rope shortened several times. But Mother was only four feet eleven, and she needed that rope longer. Finally, Pauline grew tall enough to jump up and catch hold of it. That's when Dad sealed it up. Pauline screamed for days over it."

"Where was that opening?" Amanda asked, her interest piqued. "I didn't see any."

"At the top of the stairs, above the landing."

Amanda remembered the closet ceiling, and her lower jaw dropped. "Was there ever an opening in Pauline's closet?"

"No, why do you ask?"

"Because...I'm not sure...something strange there, on the..." She let the words die.

Preston and Molly watched her. "I may be crazy, but it's a possibility." More like a certainty, she thought, and she began to smile. "I think she's in the attic," she blurted. "The opening is in her bedroom closet."

Preston jumped to his feet. "Are you sure?"

"Reasonably. That closet ceiling is done in the oddest pattern I've ever seen, for a closet." She stood ready to go.

"I hope you're right," Preston said. "Let's get over there right now."

Back at the old house, they hurried up the stairs to Pauline's room. Inside the closet, they stared at the ceiling. "That center tile doesn't quite fit right," Amanda said. "It could be the opening, though I don't see any rope to pull down the stairs."

Preston jumped to touch it. It immediately rose into place. "That's got to be it," he cried out. "Now let's see if we can find a ladder."

"I never saw one in our earlier searches," Amanda said. "What about in the garage?"

"I'll go look."

She could hear him running down the stairs as she stood looking at the center tile. Within minutes, Preston was back with a ladder. He reached the tile, and with both hands, managed to pull it away from the ceiling. Then the hidden rope dropped, and the stairs became visible.

He pushed the ladder he'd just used out of the way, then pulled down the attic ladder.

"Preston," Amanda said, "let me go up. That ladder doesn't look too strong." She pushed in front of him and started the climb. If Pauline were in the attic, she would hate it if Preston found her. As for herself, Amanda didn't care what Pauline thought.

She climbed slowly, half afraid of what she might find. When her head rose above the attic floor, she stopped and said, "The mannequins are all up here, some lying on the floor." Turning her head, she saw the bags of food scattered about, and in one corner lay a pile of unopened mail. "And her unopened mail," she added. On the final step, she saw Pauline's head poking out from under a blanket on the floor. She didn't stir, and Amanda's heart started to race.

"What's up there?" Preston demanded from behind her. He'd climbed the ladder, but couldn't quite see Pauline.

"Go get your cell phone. Call the police and an ambulance," she ordered.

"It's in the car. I'll be right back," he said. "Is Pauline OK.?"

"No, she's not." She carefully walked over to Pauline. "Pauline," she called out. Anguish wrenched at her heart. "We're here to help you." She touched Pauline's gaunt face, the flesh cold and stiff.

Lying on her back, Pauline lay finally at peace. Amanda knelt beside her. Tears came to her eyes as she looked at the wide, fixed stare on Pauline's face. "Oh, Pauline. We could have helped you, if you'd let us." Sorrow filled her, not just for Pauline, but also for Preston. He'd taken his parents' deaths so hard, what would this do to him?

"The police are on the way," Preston called from the bottom of the stairs. He climbed into the attic, rushing over to his dead sister. Amanda stood back.

"Oh, Pauline," Preston gasped. "Why did you do it?" He lowered his head and kissed her. "I should have known. I should have guessed what you were up to. Forgive me."

"You couldn't possibly have known," Amanda said, fighting back the tears. She placed her hand on his shoulder and squeezed it. "She didn't want our help."

"If I'd been more attentive, forced her to accept help."

"She wouldn't have let you."

He knelt with his head lowered for a few moments, holding one of Pauline's thin hands. A siren could be heard on the street. The ambulance parked in front of the house. Slowly, Preston got to his feet, as Amanda rushed down the stairs to open the door.

"Up in the attic," Amanda told the medics. "The opening is in the bedroom, up here." She led the way up to the closet. Preston had just come down the attic stairs, using a handkerchief to wipe away the tears.

He sat on the side of Pauline's bed, hunched over, with his hands under his armpits for warmth. The bitter cold house had the feel of a morgue. He looked up at Amanda. "She's dead."

"Yes, and so thin. Must have been starving herself a long time."

The medics overhead were talking as the two policemen came into the bedroom. They went up the ladder to the attic. Amanda sat on the bed beside Preston.

"It's all my fault," he said.

"Don't be silly, Preston. It's a tragedy you couldn't foresee. Never did she accept any help or advice from you, as you well know."

"I should have tried harder, forced help on her."

"Are you going to flail yourself over this, just as you did over your parents' accident?" This wasn't the time for anger, but she felt it just the same, though her eyes were still moist. "Preston," she said, with a kinder voice. "Don't brood over this. It won't help anyone."

Slowly and carefully, the stretcher was lowered down the stairs and out of the closet; the two officers followed.

"We need to ask some questions," one officer said. "Who is the woman, and what are your connections to her?"

Preston answered in a shaky voice. He spoke of their search for her over the past few days, and of her refusal to accept any help. Amanda added what she could, but knew little more than Preston.

"She's been living up there?" the officer asked.

Amanda nodded. "With the mannequins. Her state of mind made her think they were her friends. She's been mentally ill for years. She told us she was going to Paris for new clothes. Obviously, she didn't go. We didn't worry about her at first, until someone told us Pauline was in town."

"When did you find her?"

"Just before we called you," Preston said. He went on to tell about Pauline's activities as a child, and why the original attic opening had been closed. He didn't know about this new one until they found it minutes ago.

"We'll probably need an autopsy," the policeman said. "And you'll have to come down to headquarters and answer some questions." He nodded at Amanda. "You, too," he added.

Long after the ambulance and police were gone, Preston continued to sit on the bed, staring at the closet.

The funeral was over, and the small group moved away from the gravesite. Pauline had been buried beside her parents.

"We'll take Molly home," Hallie said to Preston, as they neared the cars. Molly had come with Preston and Amanda.

"Thanks," Preston said. He gave George a pat on the shoulder as the three walked away.

The strain of the past few weeks had ended for Molly and Hallie. They now spoke with love and respect for each other.

Preston turned to Amanda. "Let's go for coffee," he said.

She nodded as she tried to reason out how to help Preston overcome his guilt for what had happened. When they were seated in the restaurant, she said, "You know, Preston, Pauline lived a tortured life, never at home with herself, let alone others. She never would have blamed you for a thing, had she been completely normal. Her misery is ended now, and so should yours be. No purpose is served to look backward, harbor regrets, feel guilty."

He nodded and forced a smile. "You're right, but what do I have to look forward to?" He studied her face as he waited for her response.

She knew what he was driving at, but couldn't give him the answer he wanted, at least not now. "My first priority is to get that college degree. We'll figure it out from there. Maybe time will heal all the hurt. Who knows."

"And the divorce?"

She thought for a moment. "There's no hurry. That, too, can wait." She thought about Brooke's call. "Let's go see Brooke soon, and the children. Get our minds off what's happened." A tremendous relief filled her. She could make any important decisions later, with a clearer mind.

ABOUT THE AUTHOR

The author, Jean Kvavle, nee Wallace, an English Émigré, lives in the Pacific Northwest. She is a many faceted individual. In addition to her love of writing, she is addicted to gardening, fond of the beauty of nature, a dedicated bird watcher, a mother and a homemaker. Mannequins is her third book. It joins Blank Pages, and The Daffodil Orchard on a growing list of publications.

Printed in the United States
20526LVS00007B/103-126